The Road to Hell

A novel by
Harley Gamble

The Road to Hell

1

Senate Office Building, Washington, DC
Monday, December 10, 1860, 11AM

Dry kindling

Lean and tall with a shock of dark hair atop his six-foot, four-inch frame, Senator Charles Sumner extended his right hand and welcomed General Lemuel Clarkhorn into his private office. "Lemuel, my friend, welcome!"

The smiling General shook Sumner's hand before he fingered his snow-white muttonchops. As he eased into a red leather chair, he nodded toward the outer office. "Charles," he whispered, "I heard your interim receptionist was a distracting female quadroon, but I didn't know how much distraction I would see!"

"Her name is Marilee Lewallen. She's my wife's day secretary, but she's helping my here until I fill my reception position. Marilee's a skilled woman. She reads and writes, ciphers like a man, doesn't make mistakes, and will be here until I select a new aide. Perhaps a month, maybe two or more. I don't know how long it will take."

Lemuel snorted. "Another month or two, my ass! Her reading,

writing, and ciphering skills may make you think of a man, but nothing else about her will! You remain the trailblazer's trailblazer, you old fox!"

Charles said, "Marilee's more than work skills behind a pretty face and awe-inspiring body. She's the politician's dream tool, even though her mocha skin color is not. She is competent, calculating, and knows how to keep her mouth shut."

"Admirable traits...", said Lemuel.

"She also is a cold-blooded *laissez-faire* capitalist of the highest order who will do anything for money."

Lemuel's smile broadened, and a twinkle appeared in his eye. He asked, "Anything? I love it! Can I borrow her the next time my wife spends a few days with her mother?"

"Anything excludes what you want right now!" Charles chuckled under his breath. He glanced at Marilee, made sure she wasn't listening, and changed the subject. "Brr! Chilly, damnable icy rain and sleet mix today. I'd rather have snow!" He rubbed his hands together. "How about a drop of something to warm your gizzard on a miserable day?" he asked. "Nothing can match the delicate glory of Kentucky Bourbon!"

"I'll drink to that!" said Lemuel.

Charles removed a bottle and two glasses from his desk's file drawer and poured two drinks. "Here's to good Bourbon, cheap cotton, and free men where we want them."

Lemuel accepted his glass. "... And to our successful enterprise!" He drained his Bourbon in a single swallow. After a quick breathy blow, he grinned and extended his glass for more. "Silk; that is as smooth as silk."

Charles refilled Lemuel's glass and raised his own again. "I give you capitalism's holy grail and our bright future! A secure business with a hungry market that creates business and accrues usurious profits."

Lemuel touched his glass to Charles'. "I salute you! I salute you thrice. Once for the free raw materials your National Forestry Program provides us. Again, for the cheap labor the underground railroad provides us, and a third time for Colonel Elijah Spoon's security troops!"

Charles said, "... I accept a fourth salute! For a government eager to buy all the lumber we can produce at the price we name!"

Clarkhorn bowed and clicked his heels. "You are the ultimate genius, Sir, and as your willing accomplice, I salute you!" He drank his shot with a quick gulp.

Charles swallowed his bourbon as well. "How about one more?" he asked as he raised the bottle.

Lemuel smacked his lips and nodded. "That stuff is as smooth as your silver tongue during a negotiation." He chuckled under his breath as he raised a thumb to show approval.

Charles feigned a sheepish look, no small feat for one who's displays of humility were rare. He poured another drink for each of them, and added, "What I accomplished was simple and I take little credit... It was like dealing with children who will give you anything for more candy or dogs who will trade gold for bones."

Lemuel's eyes seemed to take on a reddened hue. He gulped his whisky down, grinned, and said, "Here's to nothing changing."

2

MOSES Prayer Hall, Philadelphia, Pennsylvania
Monday, December 10, 1860, 6PM

The fuse...

Atwater Coyle was a pale and thin man, almost handsome with a perfect part down the middle of his wavy black hair. His long fingers offered an affirming handshake or a steel tight grip when the need arose, and his mustache and bearded chin accented his aura. Atwater seemed a leader in a chaotic place.

Although poor in terms of silver and gold, Atwater viewed his poverty as Jesus' tool to keep him focused on his sheep, and the message that would assure their salvation. When told to simplify his life and needs, he obeyed. He pressed his pants under library books and stuffed newspapers in his pants legs and shoes to insulate his body in the winter. Aware he was a man not of, but with, God, his wealth lay in his resolve, religious dedication, and ability to proclaim the Good News.

Atwater's devotion insulated him from the slurs and ridicule of money changers and idolaters. He knew the day would come when their wealth would disappear, and he, with others so chosen, would determine every charlatan's fate.

The responsibility humbled him, but it created neither self-doubt nor fear. Atwater knew he was in the first rank of God's Christian army and defined himself by the honor his position provided. The rich men's ridicule, the opinion of fools, the book-learning Philadelphians with money and wanting more who considered him crazy, would sting a lesser man. None of it affected Atwater. He understood his power. They were not God's messengers on earth. He was, and some followers shared Atwater's passions.

Others wanted a warm place to sit on cold winter nights.

3

MOSES Prayer Hall, Philadelphia, Pennsylvania
Monday, December 10, 1860, 6:45PM

Atwater paced between his pulpit and the scattered assembly of sinners as the wind outside the Prayer hall howled and sleet banged on its walls and roof. He thought, *fifteen minutes before the evening service starts and I ain't got enough congregants to wad a shotgun.* He stopped in front of Tom Killen, bent to his friend's ear, and whispered, "The Devil's keeping people away tonight, Tom. He's doing it with weather trickery!"

The thought of satanic power hurt Atwater, and that meant the Lord hurt, too, and not just because Satan kept folks from salvation with bad weather. The *Philadelphia Daily Truth Fountain's* untrue account of life at the Callaghan Plantation in Stafford, Virginia, which wasn't that far away, also contributed. The newspaper's lying picture of a smiling Callaghan with a beautiful fancy dressed wife on his arm was bad enough. Written nonsense about his business successes and generosity was worse. Atwater knew it sickened Jesus as much as it did him.

In Atwater's heart he heard the Lord say, *Brother Coyle, Cal-*

laghan is the biggest slave owner in Virginia and this Truth Fountain story of his success and generosity is Satan's false praise. That plantation is of and by Old Billy, and that means it is of and by human bondage! The Devil is dancing on the backs of Callaghan's slaves while Philadelphia's ig'nernt newspaper readers accept these praiseful words.

Atwater sensed more wisdom would follow. He trembled; he asked, but not out loud, *"Lord... I sense you ain't alone this evening. Is it all right for me to want to know who's with you? I mean, since I'm thinkin' you want me to do something for you, I'd like to know who else is involved."*

The Lord answered in a quiet voice. "Archangel Gabriel is with me Atwater and you'll soon remember that he talked to you in your sleep last night!"

Atwater didn't remember his dream. "H-m-m-m!"

The Lord continued, "My Brother, the time for retribution is at hand." Ten seconds later, He asked, "Do you understand?"

Atwater said, "I think so, but I ain't certain." He asked himself, *Is the Lord saying it's time to cut the nuts off the hog?*

The Lord continued speaking in Atwater's heart. "My anger is greater than Satan's weather outside. Does that give you an idea of how strong my anger is?"

"It does!" answered Atwater in a voice that contained an unspoken question mark.

The Lord continued, "It's very strong. I'm calling you to do something in my name."

"I'll get my coat," said Atwater.

The Lord rebuked him. "Not right now! Soon... You'll know when."

4

**MOSES Prayer Hall, Philadelphia, Pennsylvania
Monday, December 10, 1860, 7PM**

Atwater tucked his Philadelphia *Daily Truth Fountain* in a hip pocket and opened the front door about an inch. Satan's stiff wind and sleet continued to punish the building. Although the storm tore one end of the MOSES: Men Of Strength Ending Slavery sign free as he watched, the hall stood otherwise unsullied. *We stand together,* thought Atwater. He closed the door.

Atwater learned fast and well, which was good because the service would have a late start if he took much longer. He greeted every sinner as he walked down the center aisle. Below the pulpit, he turned, saw a few strangers, and smiled. He never knew if a newcomer was a victim, a spirit, be it holy or not, or just a stranger, but tonight he looked for special guests. For the first time, he sought avenging angels prepared to offer their last full measure of devotion. Overcome, Atwater began speaking in an unknown tongue as three final pilgrims entered from the storm. Would they be Avenging Angels? He would see.

When no one else appeared, Atwater whispered to the Lord

and Gabriel, "I'll do as told. Just point me in the right direction." Then, as every Monday, Wednesday, and Friday at seven, he cleared his throat to get everyone's attention.

He thought, *I'm a man affirmed. Tonight, everything will be special,* as he climbed the steps and stood behind the dais. His mind raced. *God knows my true worth! Someday, if I continue to show my worth, he'll make me an archangel. I'd be Archangel Atwater, just like Gabriel because neither of us has a last name!* He longed for that day; the day of Archangel Atwater's second birth... and he decided a full name would make him sound more official as he looked at his congregation.

The assembled, all sinners, some drunk, some sober, most unstable, and all looking for a warm place to rest, marveled when Atwater raised both of his hands high. Five dramatic seconds later, he shouted, "Brothers, Sisters, I bring you good news. Slavery's end draws near! The Lord sent Gabriel to me as I slept last night. He got me ready, and today the Lord put two epiphanies on me; one is mine and the other His own." Atwater lowered his hands, gripped the dais, and closed his eyes for a brief prayer. When he opened them again, he chanted, "We're to help Archangel Gabriel. Archangel Michael will be there, too, some way, sometime soon!" Amid the gathered murmurs and whispers, the time for Atwater to rename himself arrived. In a voice louder and clearer than ever before, he said, "With the matter of helpin' the Archangels' asked and answered, Satan now knows the name Atwater Coyle far too well. I'm to use a new name in this mission, one befitting a Christian soldier." The drunks sobered some and the others froze in rapt silence as Atwater pointed straight up and shouted, "Gabriel himself renamed me." After another heavy silence, he rasped, "With God and Jesus' approval, of course." He snorted, caught his breath, and yelled as loud as he could, "My brothers and sisters, I stand before you as 'Saint Sword'."

Three women chanted in unknown tongues and two others twitched as Atwater entered a period of holy silence with his finger pointing high. When he spoke again, he jabbed his pointing finger up and down and trumpeted his pride in doing the Lord's will. Save for the drunks, the revelation sapped every emotion in the Prayer Hall. It exhausted most of the gathered even though the service would continue for another two hours.

As the clock by the front door struck nine, Saint Sword asked the Dinwiddie Brothers, Ed, Fulton, and Calvin, along with Tom Killen, and John Fear, to stay. He had a special message for the five of them and no one else.

The men pulled their chairs into a circle in front of the pulpit after the others left. Saint Sword made eye contact with each before saying, "My brothers, the Lord calls us to his service."

Ed Dinwiddie, the tallest, oldest, second smartest of his clan, and possessor of the best beard, asked, "Brother Coyle, I mean, Saint Sword, what is it the Lord wants us to do? Me and my brothers believe in the blood, and Tom and John do too, but why's the Lord calling the likes of us? We ain't got nothing and Calvin can hardly talk."

A benevolent smile painted Saint Sword's face. "We're going to do two things. One, we're gonna help the Archangels smite some of God's enemies, and two, we're going to free some slaves."

John Fear, the tortured possessor of a hemorrhoid in all its glory, positioned his legs and rear on a chair near Saint Sword. His weathered seventy-year-old face, almost as crimson as his veined bulbous nose, darkened as he asked, "Don't smiting mean killing?"

Saint Sword explained, "Think about freeing slaves, John... setting men free. If evil men die, it'll be on account of God wanting 'em dead, not us!" Although it looked like it to Tom Killen, Atwater didn't lick his nose before he added, "If we smite God's enemies while we do His work, it's all part of His plan." Atwater leaned closer to John to smell his breath. *Tobacco and onions,* he thought before he whispered, "Rejoice, Brother!"

A lean man with a partial beard who needed a place to prop his feet, Tom Killen considered Atwater's words before he clasped his hands over his heart. "I think I can speak for everybody when I say we're ready to answer the Lord's call." Tom thought a minute before adding, "Thing is, ain't no slaves around here…"

Saint Sword clasped a firm grip on each of Tom's shoulders. He continued, "God's sending us to a plantation in Stafford, Virginia. They's more darkies there than you can shake a stick at!"

More curious than distrustful of Saint Sword's proposal, Tom asked, "Are you sayin' we can walk in and out with more darkies than you can shake a stick at? Tell me more about that. It don't sound right."

"The Lord ain't ig'nernt, Tom!" A weary Atwater sighed, "Tom… the Lord said there's no security anywhere around that plantation and we can get in quick, load the slaves in our wagons quick, and get out quick, too."

Tom blinked. "Where we gonna take 'em?"

"That's easy!" answered Atwater. "We'll bring 'em here!"

John Fear understood. "You're saying no security means Jesus is looking out for us, but what if somebody don't get the message and starts shooting? I mean, I ain't scared, but I don't want nobody blasting at me, neither."

Saint Sword's hand clasped John's knee. "Brother Fear, I'm telling you God's armor will protect us as we do His work. As for us not being afraid," he paused and reflected before adding, "Jesus faced death on a cross without bein' afraid. We ain't facing' no cross!"

Fulton, the self-proclaimed smartest and by far the heaviest of the brothers, scratched his cherubic pink chin. After he loosened the length of Manila hemp that kept his pants up, he weighed his options. Soon, he said, "Ain't right to turn Jesus down. I'll do anything He wants."

Atwater smiled, and said, "Amen, Brother!"

Fulton mused about one of his brothers. "When we see them archangels, do you think they'll help Calvin with his talking and remembering... an' maybe straighten out that cockeye?"

"Brother Fulton, God is in this room watching you, Ed, me, John, and Tom as we sit and talk. He watches Calvin as much as he can tolerate, and that ain't always easy since he's short, unhandsome, and stupid on top of not talking plain. Don't get me wrong, ain't Calvin's fault that your Momma and Daddy, they were Elmer and Chastity, right, had Satan near 'em before she borned Calvin!"

Offense painted Fulton;s face as he proclaimed. "Jesus washed my Momma and Daddy in the blood...!"

"I ain't sayin' they done nothing wrong... I'm just talkin' what they call 'proximity' here. Bad luck bein' near the Devil, or some such. Anyhow, I know them above listen to you because you pray as good as anybody, even me... c'ept not as well as me with my connections. To help your family, I'll join your prayer for Calvin." When satifaction replace offense on Fulton's face, Atwater asked, "Can I have an Amen?"

The others spoke as one. "Amen and amen."

5

Callaghan Plantation, Stafford, Virginia
Saturday, December 15, 1860, 11:55PM

The match...

Atwater pulled the lead wagon's reins to the right and considered the possibility that he was more magi than archangel since he brought the gift of freedom. Afterward, he decided that since he was more a doer than a prayer, he'd been right all along. He smiled in the darkness. He didn't want anyone to think he was bragging as he reveled in his role and the new name that proved it: He was 'Saint Sword'.

Atwater touched his sheathed sword's hilt and thought it likely that Michael, not Gabriel, was keeping the sky clear and filled with moonlight for them tonight. Gabriel had worked a lot of hours at the Prayer Hall lately and even Archangels got tired sometime. The thrill of knowing his work soon would begin, led Atwater to pray in an unknown tongue and weep in gratitude for what the Lord put before him: an opportunity to set innocents free and slay His enemies. He stared at the lead wagon, aware that his emotions and those of the Crusaders centuries before were the same. His mind returned from his reverie when he saw a corner fencepost ahead on the left. Ten minutes later, brick towers appeared on either side of an ornate gated entryway.

Atwater raised his right hand high and signaled the wagons to stop. The moon provided just enough light for a squint at his pocket watch. It was after midnight. He thought, *"Perfect"* and rode to the gate and lifted its latch. Aware that God left it open as a sign of His ongoing approval, Saint Sword pushed the gate and rode through, ever the leader, and waved for the wagons to follow. When all were inside, Calvin Dinwiddie closed it behind them and snorted like a pig. It had been his favorite childhood mimicry. This time, it also was his signal to Saint Sword that all was well behind. They'd left nothing to raise suspicion.

When they first saw the plantation house, it was a half mile ahead on their right. Atwater opened his pocket watch again. It read 12:40. A line of decorative shrubs ingeniously hid the house's ground floor and part of the second from prying eyes; no simple task since it stood two full stories high and was longer and wider than anything Atwater could imagine, much less desire. Through the shrubs and beyond the immaculate lawn, three snow white columns flanked both sides of a tiled front porch's six framed shuttered windows. There were three on each side of the green double doors, each was twice the normal size.

Fulton Dinwiddie and John Fear dismounted and walked to Atwater's side. Fulton asked, "Where are the slaves? Are you sure the Lord's gonna help us get them out of here without no trouble?"

Saint Sword grabbed Fulton's shoulder and lectured, "We're here to free God's children **and** smite His enemies. Them what practice excess at the expense of others are God's enemies! If we can free the slaves and smite their masters, we'll glorify God to the highest! That means we clean out the house, too! You gotta remember who's thinkin' and who's listening in this operation!"

John seemed to understand better than Fulton. He said, "Saint Sword, I'm ready to set our brothers and sisters free, and if a man challenges me, I'll whip his ass good." He took a deep breath before continuing, "... but I ain't killin' no women and children! Jesus don't ask his sheep to kill women and young'uns! Now, we got something to do here and we gonna do it, but dead women and babies ain't His will."

Fulton agreed. "Daddy says you go to Hell if you kill a woman and killing a child's worse than that!"

Atwater hissed, "I should have left you dumbasses at home." His mind raced as he added, "Men, Jesus just told me to be as nice as we can. He wants you to leave your wagons here and sneak behind the house. They's likely a series of slave quarter huts. Wake the slaves up and bring them out the same way you went in."

Fulton asked, "... And what if somebody shoots at us?"

"Well, it likely won't be a woman shooting, so shoot back. Kill them before they can kill you! Just don't go to shooting unless somebody tries to shoot you." He touched each man's shoulder and promised, "We'll get out of here killing no women and children if we can." Five seconds later, he ordered, "Now, get moving!"

John and Fulton held their breath as they followed the shrub line toward the rear of the house.

Saint Sword watched them disappear. He stage-whispered, "Calvin, Ed, Tom, come up here." They came to Atwater's side, and he continued, "Ed, you and Calvin come with me. Tom, you stay with the wagons and the teams. When the slaves come up the bush line, get 'em in the wagons and keep 'em quiet. Tell 'em MOSES is here to lead them to the Promised Land."

"What if somebody starts yelling or something? They'll be skittish when they get here," asked Tom.

After tossing his handkerchief to his friend, Atwater answered, "Rag up any mouth needin' it. If that don't work, start pistol whipping! I ain't sacrificin' a flock for one out-of-control sheep."

"I don't want to kill no slave," said Tom. "You're God's messenger, not me! I'll keep 'em quiet, Saint Sword."

Atwater nodded to show he understood. He continued, "Jesus loves you, Tom. Now, when the slaves are in the wagons, signal me by lighting a coal oil lamp and waving it high. We need to see from down by the house."

In a voice that sounded heavy with moral conflict, Tom said, "I know…but, well… ."

Before Tom finished, Atwater spat, "What we're doing comes from Him talking and me listening, Tom. Sometimes we're not supposed to know everything He knows and I bow to Him! He knows everything and I don't know shit in comparison! Anyhow, He will guide and protect us through our every thought and fear so long as we do what He tells us, whether we understand or not! We're here to do His work, not make decisions! Does that he'p?"

Tom took a deep breath. He exhaled a whispered, "I'll keep the slaves quiet. What're you and the rest going to do now?"

Atwater looked at Ed and Calvin as he answered, "God ain't told me yet, but he will soon." He added to Tom, "Remember to show me the lamp when you have the slaves."

Ed and Calvin followd Atwater down the shrub line and through some pin oaks before kneeling behind a row of Rhododendrons twenty feet from the Manor's steps. As they gathered themselves, Atwater whispered, "The Lord just told me to purge Satan from this house!"

Calvin seemed to pay attention as Ed asked, "Don't purge mean throwin' up, somethin' like that?"

Atwater sighed, "Ed, in this case, it means sending the flesh merchants inside straight to Hell. They live in comfort built on the flesh and blood of others and God says he's through with stuff like that forever!"

Ed whispered, "Well, I reckon He knows, like I told you at the Prayer Hall, that I ain't killing no women... if I can get around it!"

Calvin made a sound everyone knew signaled he agreed with his brother.

Atwater groaned, "Fellers, for the last time, them people's souls ain't here no more. They died when they took their first slave. What we're doing is helping God close His book on them... which is what He wants to do." He closed the issue with, "When we go through that door, remember it was God and Jesus, not Saint Sword, who said smite 'em... and we ain't in position to take no prisoners tonight."

Behind the house, twenty pecan trees limited Fulton and John's view of three identical log cabins with heavy doors and stone chimneys. Between the cabins were horseshoe pits, clothes-lines, and plowed plots, probably for vegetables.

Fulton whispered, "Dang! That's better than home. I don't know..."

John interrupted, "... Hush! Don't think about nothing but what we're doing! Now, let's open those doors!" John tested the door of the nearest cabin and found it unlatched. He pushed it open, and the hearth's embers brightened in the new air as he stepped inside. The new light and accompanying rush of cold air awakened all ten males inside, six men and four teenage boys. John pulled Fulton inside and closed the door behind them before announcing, "Slaves of men, MOSES is here to set you free and lead you to the land of milk and honey."

Sounds of hope and disbelief filled the room. A teenage boy said, "You ain't Moses. You a Yankee."

Irritation flashed in John's voice as he chanted, "I didn't say I was MOSES, stupid! What I'm sayin' is that we're taking all of you to a new life."

A voice from the darkest far corner asked, "What the Hell's goin' on around here?" John and Fulton squinted in that direction as the voice added, "You sound like two crazy white men to me. Nobody with sense would say what you're saying, and we all know it!"

John's voice changed from irritated to angry. "Listen, dopey! This ain't us talkin' for us. God told us to free your asses and we can't do it if you don't cooperate! Now, get up, get dressed, and come on! ... and come on means right now!"

A deep voice from the other corner said, "I smell a trap to catch troublemakers! I heard somebody had one!"

Another voice, an older man's from near the hearth, asked, "How do we know you ain't settin' a fool's trap for Massa Callaghan? We ain't goin' nowhere if we ain't sure about that."

John's tone changed from anger to exasperation. "Freedom, time, and death are marching in lockstep tonight! You slaves get dressed if you're comin'! I can't prove nothin' if you just sit there!"

The men and boys stood and dressed. Fearful sounds danced through every conversation as they lined up at the door. The deepest voice spoke again. "Talk more... white man! You could be a liar and hidin' it!"

Fulton pressed his hands against his temples as he whispered, "We're abolitionists! We're risking our lives for you slaves!"

A suspicious boy asked, "How come we are so special?"

Anger leaped back into Fulton's voice as he snapped, "You are special because God chose you! You'd be shit if it wadd'n for that!" He looked up and down the line of men and boys. "Why am I the only one feeling the urgency here? I don't see nobody getting ready to run or hear nobody offerin' to help us! Somebody at least tell us about the other cabins."

The deep voice said. "You got six unclaimed women next over and two married couples with small children share the one on the other end."

Fulton asked deep voice, "What you go by?"

Deep voice, a tall, muscular man with coal black skin and graying hair answered, "Joshua, they call me Joshua."

"Joshua, if you and these gutless bastards want freedom, it's up that hill in the wagons we brought... and we are runnin' out of time."

Joshua addressed the line of slaves. "I'm goin'; if you ain't goin', go sit down." Nobody sat. He looked at the other men and boys, and added, "I'm going to roust the far cabin, and the wives there can wake the unclaimed women." He slipped through the door and looked back. He looked and sounded stern as he pointed at each slave and said, "For now, and until I say different, do what these white men say! That includes you, Andrew!"

The questioning teen hesitated. "Joshua, our life here ain't bad. If we run and get caught..."

Joshua answered, "Andrew, you are old enough to decide for yourself. If you ain't going, just sit on your bed and keep your mouth shut until Massa Callaghan finds you. Then you say whatever you need to help yourself, c'ept don't say or do nothin' to help 'em hunt the rest of us."

Andrew folded, and then unfolded, his arms before he said, "I think... I don't know what I think... but I'm going."

Minutes later, the last cabin's wives led Joshua into the unclaimed women's quarters. As the women dressed, the first cabin's line of slaves relaxed. They laughed and talked louder. Andrew took charge of the unwanted sound. "Joshua wants everybody to hush for now!"

Fulton blurted, "All of you hush!" He pointed to Andrew and added, "No slaves will give orders about nothin'! We order and you do! Understand?"

Andrew gritted his teeth as he obeyed Joshua. He nodded, but didn't answer.

Joshua opened the cabin door and shepherded six frightened young women inside. "This makes us six women, two families with two small children each, and the four boys and six men in our cabin. That's twenty-four, that's everybody, all the field hands anyway." He looked at Andrew, paused, looked at Fulton, and said, "Something's going on. What is it?"

Fulton jabbed a finger toward Joshua and said, "Andrew says you told him to have everybody hush! We give the orders, and you do what we say! It ain't no other way!" He softened his tone and almost lamented, "You darkies might get shot dead for running, but we white men are risking jail time here!" Fulton looked at his brother and saw John's facial tic coming to life. He knew to calm down for his brother's sake so he whispered, "We want to get home safe, and we can't risk getting caught because a bunch of darkies disobeyed us!"

Andrew and Joshua exchanged looks, but didn't speak. Aware that Fulton's shouting could have disturbed the house, Joshua said, "Field hands, I'm going to do what they say and anybody with second thoughts needs to sit down and stay quiet 'til we're gone. I don't want nobody goin' that won't do what they told."

Ray from the third cabin spoke up. "My wife, our children, and me, we ain't going. I don't know all the reasons we ain't, but I know we ain't." He looked at his wife and said, "We'll sit and keep the young'uns quiet."

Ed answered. "MOSES don't want nobody comin' that's heart

ain't in it. We'll leave you now. Good luck to you."

Fulton said, "... Everybody, take two minutes to make sure they got what they really, really gotta have and no more. We're traveling light and fast."

As the slaves separated to gather and pare down what they needed, John asked, "Joshua, the big house..."

"I can get you in it... three men in there'll kill you if they can: Massa Douglas, Mister Philip, he's about twenty, and Jerome. Jerome's the house boss; he must be seventy and he loves the Callaghans. He's good with a gun, too. I saw him shoot once."

"How about women? Do any inside know how to handle a weapon?"

"You got four all together; three ain't dangerous. You got Miss Angela, she is about fourteen, her momma Mrs. Lucy, and Martha Anne, who does a little cleaning and cooking. Arthritis done eat Martha Anne up, but she stays because Mrs. Lucy loves her. Martha Anne helped raise her as a child... now, the fourth woman is the dangerous one. She's a yellow girl about fifteen, with red hair, blue eyes, and a full-grown woman's body. In the house, they call her Mary. Out here, we call her Mary Magdalene."

Fulton said, "My churchin' tells me a lot by the name you call her..."

"Mary draws pictures, laughs girl laughs with Miss Angela, and keeps her messes picked up in the daytime. When Miss Angela goes to bed, Mary don't go to the room she shares with Martha Anne; she goes to Mister Philip's room. She keeps his bed warm, if you know what I'm sayin'." Fulton gasped and Joshua continued, "Massa Douglas knows about it but he won't send Mary to the fields unless Miss Angela finds out her yellow girlfriend entertains her brother at night. If Miss Angela don't know nothin', Mister Douglas looks the other way because Mary keeps Philip under control, keeps him thinking about what's between her legs instead of getting grabby around suitable young women. Philip, he's a wild one."

"His Momma… I can't believe she'd tolerate that in her house."

"Miz Lucy, she sees what she wants to see. That means she doesn't know nothing, and she don't want to know nothing, either. That's the way she gets along. As far as she's concerned, if she don't see it or hear about it, it ain't there."

Fulton gestured for the slave line at the door to be quiet. He whispered, "Go through the pecan trees and stay in the shadows until you are on the road. A man named Tom is waiting for you there with two wagons. They'll take you to freedom."

Fulton pulled one of the two pistols in John's belt free and handed it to Joshua. He laid a hand on John Fear's shoulder, and said, "The Lord is helping us and Joshua here's his instrument." John didn't answer. The field hands walked toward the trees and made their way to the wagons.

Fulton said, "Joshua, I want you to meet some friends of John's and mine. They're waiting for us at the front door. Together, we will cleanse Satan from this house. Tell them everything you know about what's inside."

Joshua followed Fulton and John along the shrub line until they raced across the lawn and kneeled beside the Rhododendron hiding Atwater, Ed, and Calvin. Fulton gasped for breath before he said, "All the field hands should be at the wagons by now."

Atwater looked at the road and saw the lantern. He turned to Fulton and asked, "… And exactly who is your slave friend, Fulton? What the Hell are you thinkin'?"

Joshua whispered, "My name is Joshua."

Atwater ignored Joshua and gripped Fulton's forearm. He said through clinched teeth, "Only a crazy man would give one of them a gun and bring him to God's serious doings!"

Fulton tried to explain. "Joshua ain't no regular slave. The others listen to him, and he knows everything there is to know about this house."

Atwater snorted, "Fulton, it's a big square house with big square rooms! We don't need no slave to tell us that!"

Fulton shook his head from side to side as he explained, "Saint Sword, Joshua knows who in there can make trouble for us and who can't. He knows where everybody is right now, too!" Fulton took a deep breath. "He wants to be free, and I respect him enough to let him carry a pistol."

Atwater stared at Joshua in silence. He asked, "Did they tell you about MOSES?"

"They said it meant, 'Men of Strength Ending Slavery'. They said you from Philadelphia and this is your first abolition raid."

Atwater sighed. He shrugged, and said, "Long as you're here, tell us everything you know about that house, including who and where."

Joshua did and Atwater absorbed every detail before deciding, "This ain't going to be hard. If the Lord will send the men out for a look after we go through that door, they'll be easy pickin'. We'll have to go get 'em up and downstairs if they don't, so let's hope they get curious."

Joshua whispered, "Getting in… if Jerome followed his routine, and he always does, we're looking at a locked front door…"

"Can you open it?"

"No," answered Joshua as he slowly shook his head from side to side. "Everything Mister Callaghan buys is the best there is, and that includes his locks. You'll have to shoot the door open."

Atwater nodded, and said, "Ed, the Lord is tired of waiting. Put your shotgun in the keyhole and blow that lock out of there!"

They crept onto the porch; Ed looked at Atwater and touched the end of his shotgun's barrel to the lock. He fired. Wood splinters flew into the house and the lock separated and hung from the now open door.

6

Callaghan Plantation, Stafford, Virginia
Sunday, December 16, 1860, 12:30AM

The Flame...

Saint Sword kicked the door open, and all five raced inside.

A voice to their left roared, "What's going on here? Throw them guns down!"

Ed, closest to the voice on the left end of the MOSES line, swung his shotgun toward the voice. He fired his second blast while shouting, "Abolition, house slaves! MOSES sets you free!"

He never saw Jerome, who'd stepped behind a marble inlaid plaster wall an instant before Ed's shotgun burst two low burning ornate oil lamps and a bust of Napoleon Bonaparte. One lamp fell near Jerome's feet, causing Jerome to curse for the first time in years, and he kicked it into a corner where the rest of the oil poured, and visible fingers of blue flame raced across the floor.

Jerome gripped his revolver in both hands and entered the foyer before shooting. His first shot shattered Ed's chest, causing the Abolitionist to drop his now empty shotgun, and a second tore through Ed's neck and ricocheted off a marble column before rupturing Calvin Dinwiddie's liver. Jerome's third shot separated the back of Ed's skull from his face and his remaining neck, strewing tissue and bone over Saint Sword and Jerome. Ed turned toward Atwater and seemed to concentrate through empty eyes. He smiled as he took a single step and fell dead.

As Ed fell, his brother Calvin did something he'd never done before. He screamed while kneeling prayerfully. A confused Atwater saw Jerome's Colt flash again, creating an eerie scene in which a black man in a flaming room shoots at the Abolitionists who save him! The Lord told Atwater that the man shooting from the fire was a demon. Saint Sword screamed, "Satan; Lucifer!" as he fired his Colt at the now burning black man. Jerome died instantly as the bullet struck him between the eyes.

… A rifle fired and echoed from somewhere upstairs. Another rifle loosed five shots in quick succession from the far-right corner on the ground floor. One shot, nobody ever knew who fired it, burst John Fear's heart.

Joshua took the pistol from the dead man's hand and screamed, "We're sitting ducks out here! They're shooting from both up and downstairs! That last one came from overhead by the sittin' area and railing! Other'n was from Massa Callaghan's bedroom in the far-right corner!"

Douglas Callaghan closed his bedroom door. As he reloaded his rifle, he told his wife, "Lucy, they're not thieves! They're abolitionists and Joshua's with them. I recognize his voice. They're trying to kill us, burn us out!" He opened the back window and said, "Come here, Lucy; I want you to jump down and run into the pecan trees! Don't look back until you get to the field hand cabins!"

She nodded. Her voice quivered as she asked, "Douglas, what about the children? How can we get them outside, save them?"

"I can do that alone better than we can together. I'd worry

about you as much as what I had to do. That means you have to go! Jump for me, Lucy. Do it now."

In shock, she put on her housecoat, took a new pair of shoes in one hand, and laid a quilt she'd made over an arm. Lucy jumped.

Douglas watched her run to safety before he closed the window and tucked the Starr revolver he kept by the bed in his belt. He crawled to the kitchen door, cracked it open, and looked for motion. The room was quiet, empty, and smoke free.

He hurried to the door between the kitchen and the dining room and lay down. He rolled under the dining room table, where he had a clear view of the living room and the foyer. A churning flame near Jerome's quarters lit more than just the entryway; it exposed two prone dead men and a third kneeling, praying as fate pulled him from life to death.

Gunshots echoed from somewhere, maybe upstairs, maybe down. It didn't matter where; the sounds told Douglas at least two and perhaps three intruders remained alive in the house.

Douglas rested the Starr against the dining room table leg and squinted in the heat and rising smoke. He saw no movement, no ready targets as he analyzed his threats. "Lucy's safe; Philip's tough and resourceful and Angela's scared to death. I go for her first."

A rifle fired, and the shot echoed in the foyer. As he looked to the front door, two figures darted across Douglas' line of vision in opposite directions.

Saint Sword went outside, and the other limped and groaned toward the ground floor guest room. He decided against worrying about the runner and entered the hallway. He followed a fire-lit trail of fresh blood to the guest room door and pressed an ear against it. He heard nothing, then a cough and a faint moan.

Douglas tucked the Starr in his belt and touched his Remington to the door. It resisted; he kicked it. When the door flew open, he saw a blood-soaked Fulton Dinwiddie sitting on the bed.

Fulton forced himself to stand. He weaved, gripped the headboard to keep from falling and screamed, "Satan, I purge this Hell of you and your kind!"

Douglas raised his Remington toward Fulton's face and asked, "Who are you and where'd you come from?"

"I'm an Archangel! God sent to set men free!"

Douglas said, "If it works out, you'll never know it." He shot Fulton two inches above the bridge of his nose and whispered, "Archangel, my ass!" He left the room and closed the door.

Flames licked through every window on the front of the house as Douglas raced to the stairway and climbed. As he turned at the halfway switchback landing, a shot from somewhere below shattered his right shoulder. Douglas fell against the wall behind him. His shoulder seemed on fire, but the pain couldn't keep him from focusing his eyes on a man below, a man partially hidden by smoke and fire.

In the foyer below, Joshua pointed to Douglas and shouted, "Prepare for Jesus, Massa Callaghan! Your slavin' days are done!"

Philip's Remington rifle silenced that threat from the second story's open sitting area with a shot that struck Joshua's knee; the ex-slave's collapse, painful as it was, saved him from Philip's second shot, which would have struck his heart had he still stood. Bleeding and on fire, Joshua knew his life would soon end, but in the last act of heroic defiance, he willed his Colt toward the platform above and shot Philip Callaghan dead.

Behind Philip, a frantic female voice screamed, "No, you killed Philip, you bastard! He dead!"

In the fire, a dying Joshua slid a few feet back and sat with his back against the wall. When his pants ignited, he thought it strange that his charring flesh no longer hurt as he glared into the upper area. He recognized a woman holding a rifle and laughed, "Mary Magdalene, Mary Magdalene, them big tits and that round ass have saved you for the last time. Your sugar white boy is dead and now you just another field hand. Soon you be a dead one."

Clinging to the stair rail, Douglas struggled to concentrate... Mary being alive in the sitting area probably meant Angela was not in immediate danger. He looked down, saw the crazed, dangerous, and dying Joshua sitting against the wall and laughing. Douglas thought aloud, "I need to kill that bastard before he kills me." He let his numb right arm hang free as he groped for his revolver with his left and braced himself against the now burning stair rail. He aimed the Starr at Joshua. They locked eyes and Douglas shouted, "I'm crippled, but you're dead"

Another rifle shot rang out from the sitting platform before he could fire. Douglas watched Joshua's chest explode and his torso seem to float until it lay prone on the floor.

In the smoke, Douglas couldn't see that Joshua's eyes had moved to the upstairs platform, nor could he see Joshua's Colt until he fired and burst Mary's sternum by the railing overhead.

Douglas quickly fired twice more; one shot struck Joshua's chest and the other his abdomen. Joshua glanced at the stairway, but his actual interest was in the traitorous Mary. He spat blood in her direction and laughed. "You good as gone, whore! You gonna die with your slaving devil!"

Mary touched the hole in her chest. It was big, it should have hurt, but she looked peaceful when she released the rail and touched it. She fell after losing her balance, and landed on the hardwood floor below, where a broken neck ended her concern about the painless hole between her breasts.

Mary lay dead close to Joshua. He reached for her with both

hands, but the fire was stronger than he was. He died in that position, grotesquely frozen as in stone.

Douglas looked down at Mary's twisted head and now burning body. Allowing his son to use her had shamed him, but she'd kept Philip under control around their friends' daughters. Douglas willed his way up to Angela's bedroom. He felt relief and then distress when he touched her doorknob; it was cool... and locked. He called through the door; there was no answer, so he kicked it hard to no avail. He screamed, "Angela, talk to me! Are you in there? Angela, its Daddy!"

He heard her desperate answer, "Daddy? Daddy! I'm coming!"

The door opened; Angela fell into her father's arms and sobbed, "Oh, Daddy, you're shot... and the fire! What's happening to us?"

He entered the room, closed her door behind them, and said in a forced calm voice, "I'm fine, but the fire is bad! We need to get outside."

"Daddy, what..."

"Some crazy men tried to hurt us, but they're all either dead or gone now." He tousled her hair, and said, "I want you to put on a shirt, britches, and some heavy boots for me..."

She dressed quickly, smiled through what seemed some false courage, and asked as she spun in a tight circle, "Is this good enough?"

Douglas nodded. He felt the door again. It was much hotter. The fire was close. He said, "We'll go from here to the kitchen and then into the yard."

Angela looked at the smoke curling under her door. "What if it's too hot?"

He hoped against hope. "It's hot, but not so hot we can't get through. Do you have any bathing or drinking water up here?"

"Martha Anne brought a gallon for my wash bowl before bedtime, but I haven't used it yet." She blurted, "Momma! Where's Momma? Where's Philip? What about Mary, Jerome, and Martha Anne?"

Her father answered. "Momma's outside. She's fine." He spread Angela's blanket on the floor and emptied the washbowl on it before adding, "We'll wrap the blanket around us and I'm going to cover your head while we go to the kitchen. We'll go as fast as we can and still be safe. All you have to do is stay calm and right beside me, no matter what."

Angela seemed to force another smile. "I understand Daddy." When her father wrapped the soaked blanket around them, she whispered, "I'm ready!"

Douglas touched the door again; it was hotter than before. Heat painted his face as he pulled the door ajar and led Angela into the hallway. They groped down the now smoke-filled stairway and soon passed a charred and rigid Joshua; his extended arms still pointing to Mary. Douglas held his breath and his eyes burned as he and Angela walked near Philip. When they reached the kitchen door, he shouted, "We're in the kitchen! We'll be outside in less than a minute!"

7

Callaghan Plantation, Stafford, Virginia
Sunday, December 16, 1860, 12:35AM

Aftermath...

Atwater didn't want anybody at the wagons shooting him, so he held his sword high as he ran through the shrubs. He saw Tom Killen and shouted, "Turn them wagons, Tom! We gotta get out of here right now!"

A wild-eyed Killen knew something had gone wrong, but not exactly what. He stood in his wagon's seat and sobbed, "Saint Sword, what happened down there? Where's all our MOSES brothers? Look at that damned house! Fire's coming out the roof and the shooting, the gunfire...!"

Atwater voice trembled. "The Devil done trapped us! He was waiting in there! The Dinwiddie boys, all three of them, are deader'n doornails! John Fear and a darkie who tried to help us, too! John for sure and the darkie was right behind! They's demons, Tom! Demons in a bath of blood and fire! We gotta go before they come after us! Let's get us and these slaves out of here!"

Tom pulled his reins hard left and shouted, "Gee!" He pointed to the second wagon and continued, "Anybody what can drive a team, grab them reins and follow us right now!"

As both teams lurched toward the main road, Atwater buried his face in his hands and wept. "God thinks we failed Him, Brother Tom. I mean, at least one of us failed him, and He let Satan sucker punch us for punishment."

Shocked, Tom asked, "Are you sayin' somebody in MOSES abominated?"

Atwater shook his head. "Couldn't be nothin' else! There is or was evil amongst us!"

Tom looked confused and aghast. "Can't be no abominators in MOSES! We all washed in the blood, c'ept for Calvin and he don't count!"

Atwater waved for Tom to strike the team again and answered, "… had to be at one time, Tom!" The team lathered, but Atwater told Tom to whip them again and the second wagon kept pace close behind.

8

**Callaghan Plantation, Stafford, Virginia
Sunday, December 16, 1860, 12:40AM**

Angela leaped through the kitchen door an instant before her father heard and turned to face a harsh and loud cracking sound. A huge overhead beam separated from the ceiling and fell on Douglas Callaghan. The blow was perfect. Three inches away in any direction and Callaghan would have joined his family; stunned, but alive. Instead, he died where he fell, three feet from the kitchen door and safety.

Once in the trees, Angela turned and stared as the only home she'd known burned to the ground. She cried, "Daddy, where are you? Daddy, Momma and Philip? ...Jerome? Martha Ann?"

Lucy called through the heat and the sound of their burning home, "I'm with Ray and his family! They stayed with us." She enveloped Angela in her arms and whispered, "Angela, thank God you're alive! Where are your father and Philip? Did they get out, too? Jerome, Mary, my sweet, wonderful Martha Ann... are they safe?"

Angela sobbed into her mother's ear. "Daddy was right behind me. But I don't know where he is! He pushed me through the door. I know Philip is dead. Mary's dead, too… both were on the balcony over the foyer. Jerome and Martha Anne, I know Jerome died getting us the time we needed to fight and live." She paused before adding, "I never saw Martha Anne…"

Lucy collapsed by Ray and Bitsy's doorway. She sobbed. "Who would do anything like this to us? We're good people, a Christian family that leads good lives and gives to the church and a lot of charities!" She folded her arms tightly and wailed with wide eyes, "Why, why, where's Douglas…? And who would harm Jerome and Martha Anne? He was wonderful, and Martha Anne was as much a momma to me as my real momma! I loved her!"

Ray wanted to help explain. He answered. "Miz Lucy, it was false Christians that come here. They say they Moses! I knew they wadd'n Jesus' men as soon as I heard them talk. I told 'em me, Bitsy, and the boys are stayin'! I was afraid they might kill us on the spot, but they didn't."

Bitsy asked, "Ray, what they mean when they said Moses?"

Ray answered, "I got no idea. That just what they say."

With her eyes still flooded, a trembling Lucy asked aloud, "What will we do?" Her mind raced as she added, "We were good to all our slaves… and to everybody else, too!"

Angela rested her head on the nape of her mother's neck. "Except for Ray's family, they all betrayed us."

***

Lucy wept more, but her mind hardened, as she said, "Right now, I think Douglas is with Philip and Angela is even more frightened than I am." After a pause, she added, "Tonight we sleep in the unclaimed women's beds."

Angela asked, "And tomorrow… ?"

"Tomorrow we'll move in with our friends, the Sullivans. We will plan our future there, among those who hold us dear." She kissed her daughter's cheeks and was careful not to say she would sell everything and move far away.

9

**MOSES Prayer Hall, Philadelphia, Pennsylvania
Monday, December 17, 1860, 10PM**

Unintended consequences...

Fright, exhaustion, and darkness shrouded Atwater and Tom as Tom urged their team behind the Prayer Hall. After Atwater jumped to the ground, he cupped his hands and stage-whispered to both wagons, "You darkies line up down here and stay quiet. When I say so, we'll go in that building..."

Tom counted the line and told Atwater, "Not countin' the one that went to the house and the family that stayed, my adding shows nineteen."

Atwater whispered, "Nineteen out of a crowd like that is pretty good." He pointed to the Prayer Hall and told the newly free slaves, "We wait here while my friend unhitches the teams and takes care of them. No talkin'!"

A voice from in front of the second wagon said, "I can help him... with the animals, I mean."

Atwater sighed, "He don't need no help," and walked to Tom. "Tom, hide the wagons first because we'll have police and God knows who else lookin' for 'em soon enough, includin' here. We can't look suspicious."

The words seemed to frighten the slaves even more; most knew the arson and killing that freed them assured bloodhounds and a hangman's noose were pursuing them. They were bound by fear, together and alone in a strange place. When one murmured, "We should'a stayed with Ray and Bitsy; they did the right thing," Several others agreed.

Tom heard every word. The black folks' fear frightened him as well. He went to Atwater and whispered, "Saint Sword, whatever the Lord wants us to do, we need to do it! They are getting regretful. I think they'll kill us, run for it, or get us caught."

Atwater understood. He said, "Jesus prepared me for this, Tom. They's a Senator in Washington named Charles Sumner. The *Truth Fountain* says he has helped darkies get to freedom but he don't admit nothin' for what they call 'political and legal' reasons."

Tom's face said he never heard of political or legal reasons. He nodded. "I think I've heard of him…"

"What's important here, Tom, is that me and Jesus know Sumner is the strongest voice for abolition in the whole Congress." Atwater whispered, "I heard he would have saved John Brown if he could…"

Tom whispered, "Thank you, Jesus, for a man like that!"

Atwater continued, "Paper said he has a camp in Massachusetts, outside a place called North Adams that has a water-powered sawmill." He softened his voice, "… and escaped darkies chop trees in the National Park the mill borders and cut planks the mill sells to the Interior Department. The runaways get money for their work instead of doin' stoop field work for nothin'."

Tom nodded. "I hope he pays them good. Sawmillin's hard

work, harder than field work, and you can cut a finger off before you know it!"

Atwater agreed. "That's true, but the money they'll make probably compensates for maybe missing a finger someday…"

Tom considered the business in a little more detail. "How come he gets to sell National Park trees to the Interior Department as lumber? Ain't he selling the Government wood it already owns?"

Atwater explained, "It's what you call business, Tom! What with the man being chairman of the Senate Committee that oversees the parks, there ain't likely to be no nonsense about wood coming off public land."

Tom looked confused as he returned to his original concern. "Lord, please have him want our darkies up there."

Atwater smiled. "I join you in that prayer, Brother Tom! We got nineteen slaves we need to move on to avoid a mess that ain't of our making. I ain't complaining but somebody above us either punished us for our sins, or Gabriel didn't deliver information as specified… that would be to us. Ain't no reason for them three Dinwiddie boys and John Fear to be dead because of somethin' that ain't their fault! Just makes me sick. Jesus loved them boys! I did, too!"

Tom looked pensive. "We need to tell Mr. and Mrs. Dinwiddie ourselves; don't want 'em learning from nobody else… John's wife, I mean widow, too!" He took a breath. "If I'd known they would die, and we'd kill some women, maybe kill 'em anyway… well."

Atwater soothed his friend. "Tom, right now, Saint Sword is telling you doin' God's work cost us plenty, but we did what He wanted! We freed 'em and brought 'em here because that's what He wanted! We did it for Him!" He leaned near Tom and whispered, "Be proud of what you did for Jesus…"

Tom folded his arms. "Atwater. The Lord named you 'Saint

Sword' because you can cut to the truth and explain what the rest of us need to know… you just did it again!"

Saint Sword smiled. "Jesus did that, Brother Tom. I ain't nothin' but the pipe he pours the wisdom we need through. I will say it makes me proud to serve Him that way."

Tom's attention returned to the runaways, and he called aloud, "You ex-slaves, we're going to feed everybody and then you need to sleep. We've cots for the women and small children, and extra blankets for the men, in a storage room off the Prayer Hall. Everybody'll have to sleep in the same room and keep quiet for a while, maybe a week. If the wrong people find you, they'll hang everybody, includin' all of you. I assure you, quiet and crowded beats noisy and hanged every time… now, if anybody has a question, go on and ask it. You ain't likely to get another chance." A heavy silence followed. Atwater then said, "Everybody remember that this is temporary. You ain't spending the rest of your life here." The slaves responded with an approving murmur, and Atwater continued, "Now, I'm off to arrange for your transportation to a place where you men can work, and you women can take care of your families without of being afraid of nobody."

Atwater raised both hands over his head and said, "Now, smile! God wants you to smile and thank Him for your freedom and your new life."

They did.

Atwater pointed toward the Prayer Hall, and said, "Everybody, go settle in while I plan for my journey tomorrow… a journey to set in motion the last leg of your trip to God's bounty."

As the slaves gathered their cots and blankets, Tom said, "Saint Sword, Washington's a hundred and thirty cold miles from here and that North wind will cut you up."

Atwater was confident. "I ain't worried about none of that."

Tom answered, "I'll have Darby saddled and waiting for you. He's the strongest we got. If you leave before dawn, he'll have you in Washington by late afternoon."

10

Senate Office Building, Washington, DC
Tuesday, December 18, 1860, 4:15PM

Paved with good intentions...

The icy wind blowing over the Tidal Basin tore at Atwater's coat. He shivered up the Senate Office Building steps and felt relief when he closed its heavy bronze and glass door behind him. A guard standing near the door smiled as Atwater said, "I'm here to see Senator Sumner, Senator Charles Sumner. Will you direct me to his office?"

The Guard pointed up behind Atwater. "Take that stairway. He's on the second floor, third door to your left." Before Atwater could beam a winning smile and offer a 'Much oblige!' the Guard continued, "Sumner's a tough one. If you don't have an appointment, you won't see him. I see more folks coming down disappointed from his office than any of the others."

Atwater walked to the stairs without another word. He knew that warning didn't include him because, as he thought, 'The Lord has made me known to the senator. I know in my bones he's expecting me.'

Atwater tapped on Sumner's office door once and pushed it open to expose a filled reception area. Seven men and two women occupied every couch and chair. He walked to the receptionist, a young and beautiful woman with pale mocha skin in a modest yet feminine dark blue dress. Carefully brushed waves of long black hair caressed her neck and shoulders and her dark eyes almost flashed. As she smiled, she showed the straightest, most perfect, brightest white teeth Atwater could imagine.

In an angel's voice, she said, "Good morning, Sir. Can I help you?"

Atwater read 'Marilee Lewallen,' on her desk nameplate before introducing himself. "Good afternoon, Miss Lewallen. I'm Atwater Coyle and I've an urgent matter to discuss with the senator."

She gestured toward the room and extended a smile that filled Atwater's soul before she answered. "So do these people, Mister Coyle. If you don't have an appointment, you'll have to wait your turn… you are number ten today. I'll enter your name for you. It's the best I can do."

Her words confused Atwater; *She thinks I'm just a person, not the Lord's messenger.* He decided she needed a prompt, so he leaned near her ear and whispered, "I'm God's messenger."

Marilee's smile disappeared and Atwater sensed she now looked through rather than at him as she explained, "As are many others in this room, Mister Coyle. I can make you an appointment for next week or you can wait for your turn. I've no other options for you."

Atwater thought, *this woman don't know Jesus.* Before he could speak the inner office door opened. A tall man with sideburns and a Patrician's air stepped into the reception area. The man smiled at Marilee and asked, "Miss Lewallen, who is next?"

Atwater never saw Charles Sumner before, but he knew the

Lord just stood the senator before him. Before Marilee could an-
swer, he blurted, "Senator, I've a matter of utmost urgency, and I
desperately need your help. I'm Saint Sword the Hero of Stafford,
Virginia!" He talked faster as he explained, "My earthly name is
Atwater Coyle, but in our abolitionist movement, we call it MO-
SES, I'm Saint Sword!"

"Go on…"

"The Lord used me, us really, to free some slaves in Virginia.
We still got 'em and we're on the verge of being in big trouble. We
need help."

Sumner said, "Miss Lewallen, give the other petitioners ap-
pointments for later in the week." He stepped into his office as he
said, "Mister Coyle, if you'll join me…"

Charles closed the door behind them, walked behind his desk,
and sat down. He stared at Atwater, pointed to a chair, and said,
"Sir, I've read accounts of an event in Stafford, Virginia. Were you
involved?"

Atwater liked Sumner calling him 'Sir', but he decided a senator would trust him more if he knew they both were honest-to-God
thinkers. He chose his words carefully as he said, "My MOSES
brothers and me went to Stafford to set some of God's children
free. Five good men died freeing nineteen slaves."

"… This was at the Callaghan Plantation, was it not?"

Atwater exclaimed, "It was, and I need to get rid of those darkies before they get me caught… I know people are lookin' for
them, and that means they are lookin' for me, too! They're lookin'
all over!"

Charles pressed, "Did you burn the house, kill the owner and
his son among others, and convey the slaves, the owner's legal
property, out of state?"

Surprised to hear about the owner, Atwater sighed, "… Didn'

know about the Big Slaver. We did it all, but we just come for the darkies. The rest, we didn't start it, but we did the Lord's work when he called on us. We did his will under circumstances you can't imagine!"

Sumner leaned back and raised his eyebrows in false admiration. "I prodded you to determine your dedication, Sir. We are kindred spirits."

"I'm kind of surprised that word of our rescue got around so fast."

Charles paused before adding, "Mister Callaghan had friends in Washington. He and they were birds of a feather and will be until the Audubon's cease considering buzzards as birds."

Atwater didn't know what that meant.

Sumner continued, "Callaghan's vermin friends are among our most brilliant haters of black folk. They all have full access to those that share their view in the Criminal Insurrection Department..." He smiled. "... Other than MY friends in CID's Newly Freed Citizens' Division. I must add, had some of Douglas Callaghan's cronies seen and somehow identified you, you would be in jail instead of here right now." He chuckled. "Since I chair their Senate oversight committee, they answer to me. I assure you, only a few over there would risk farting without my permission."

Atwater's spirits lifted. He whispered, "Thank you, Jesus!"

The senator waxed serious and continued, "So, Mister Coyle, how can I relieve your worries? How may I help a noble man such as you?"

Atwater stammered, "I read a story that said you had a lumber camp in Massachusetts... a camp that took in darkie runaways, offered 'em honest work and safety." He blurted, "My runners, the sooner they're gone, the better as far as I'm concerned... I don't want to hear no more about 'em after they go, either!"

The senator asked, "Where are our pilgrims right now?"

"Right now, they're at our Prayer Hall in Philadelphia. All of them are in one room and it's tight as Dick's hatband in there."

Charles feigned thought. After finger-tapping his desk for a few seconds, he whispered, "I assume they're willing to work..."

"These were field hands. Work doesn't frighten them; they love it!"

Charles poured each of them some water before he said, "Mister Coyle, I will take your darkies to my lumber mill. If they will work as hard as you say, they'll earn as much money as any white man would." He took a map from his center desk drawer. He scanned it before asking, "Can you have them at the Philadelphia Freight Depot Saturday morning at One AM?"

"They'll be there one way or another..."

Charles nodded. "A locomotive with two passenger cars bearing 'North Adams Lumber' on its boiler will be near Canterbury Road at the Depot's far north end." Sumner let his words sink in before he added, "Hide your runaways in the bushes on the Canterbury side of the tracks and go alone to speak to the engineer. Tell him my name and that you have nineteen to travel."

"Then bring 'em across?"

"He'll tell you when and how. Just do as he says. Questions?"

"Only how'd rail service get to a town like North Adams from Philadelphia?"

Charles smiled. "Mister Coyle, you needed transportation, and the Lord provided it. I thank Him for allowing me to help you when you feared you were alone!"

Atwater sighed, "Thank you, senator, and thank you, Jesus!" He jumped to his feet and added, "God bless you, senator! Between us, we gonna save these black folk and I'm gonna go home and get 'em ready!" Atwater then raced from Sumner's office and down the stairs. He left the office and reception area doors open in his haste and glee.

Marilee Lewallen closed the outer door before she looked into Sumner's private office. She asked, "Shall I close this for you, Sir?"

Charles smiled, "Leave it open, my dear… and let me ask you a question. Does Mister Coyle's appearance remind you of anyone? Think for a moment. I want to know if you saw what I did."

She didn't hesitate. "The man is a dead ringer for my favorite actor… your friend John Wilkes Booth. The resemblance is uncanny! They could be the same person! I was going to ask you the same question."

11

Freight Depot, Philadelphia, Pennsylvania
Saturday, December 22, 1860, 12:45AM

Tom pulled the wagon off Canterbury Road behind a row of wild brush. All was silent. He nodded to Saint Sword, who confirmed that they were safe and well-hidden from the train ahead and any prying eyes that may lurk behind them.

Atwater walked north on Canterbury to get a better look at the engine and two passenger cars far across the ribbons of tracks. The boiler read North Adams Lumber. He watched it belch occasional smoke puffs before returning to the wagon. He whispered, "Everything looks good, Brother Tom. I'm goin' across and check in with the engineer now."

Tom said, "... Some darkies are fidgeting."

Atwater said, "We don't need that!" He darted across the tracks and hissed up to the engineer's compartment, "Charles Sumner sent me with nineteen souls for you to take to North Adams."

The engineer, an enormous man, looked down at Atwater and then at his watch. "I'm going to raise the fire in my boiler now. You'll have about a minute to get 'em in the cars after I whistle

three long and shorts because I'll be rolling and I ain't doin' nothin' that won't look right to another railroad man! If you understand, get your ass away from my train before somebody sees you!
That means now!"

Atwater returned to Tom and the slaves. He and Tom readied
their runaways for their ride and sent them to the train when the
whistle sounded at 1:03. The slow runners entered the passenger
cars at 1:04, less than thirty seconds after the giant wheels spun
without gripping the rails. The runaways sat in silence until the
wheels caught the track on their third spin and lurched forward.
As they moved, some ex-slaves laughed aloud, and others only
smiled. The North Adams Lumber's steam locomotive departed
right on time.

12

**MOSES Prayer Hall, Philadelphia, Pennsylvania
Saturday, December 22, 1860, 1:45AM**

Atwater and Tom sat across from one another at the Prayer Hall's kitchen table. Neither man spoke until Atwater whispered, "A sip of that Communion wine would be pleasant right now. I don't think Jesus would mind if we partook of a drop or two."

Tom answered, "If we need a special occasion, we got a couple of them! One, the darkies are gone and two, they ain't gonna get us arrested."

Atwater asked, "Can I get an Amen?" as he walked to the cabinet.

Tom answered, "Amen and I want a bucket-sized glass!"

Saint Sword turned to his friend, jug in hand. "Tom, Just as Jesus turned water into wine when he thought the time was right, I know he thinks our time is right, too!" He filled two glasses and added, "I say we offer a toast not only to Jesus but also our dear departed Ed, Fulton, and Calvin Dinwiddie and John Fear... all of whom He nestles in His bosom as we speak."

13

MOSES Prayer Hall, Philadelphia, Pennsylvania
Sunday, December 23, 1860, 10AM

Tom Killen threw the Prayer Hall's kitchen door open, and all but leaped inside before he could catch his breath. He unfolded his copy of the Daily Truth Fountain so that Atwater could read the twenty-point headline. It screamed:

December 20, 1860
The once and future United States of America

Revelation, Chapter 6, verses 7-8
Holy Bible, King James Version

7. And when he had opened the fourth seal, I heard the voice of the fourth beast say, Come and see. 8. And I looked, and behold a pale horse; and his name that sat on him was Death, and Hell followed with him. And power was given unto them over the fourth part of the earth, to kill with sword, and with hunger, and with death, and with the beasts of the earth

14

Senate Office Building, Washington, DC
Monday, April 3, 1865, 9AM

John Wilkes Booth was on time for his nine o'clock appointment with Charles Sumner. He entered as the floor clock sounded its last chime and Marilee Lewallen greeted him. "Good morning, Mister Booth; you're right on time for your nine o'clock with the senator!"

Booth didn't gawk like men seeing Marilee for the first time; she'd mesmerized him twice before. He answered, "Good morning, Miss Lewallen! I hope Charles still has time for me this morning."

A voice from Sumner's private office called, "Marilee, please show Mister Booth in."

She did so and closed Charles' door after the senator's guest entered.

Sumner removed a bottle of Bourbon from his bottom right-side drawer and set it and two glasses on his desk. He looked at Booth over the glass and bottle and smiled. "You look like you could use an eye-opener. I know to Hell I could!"

Booth nodded his approval. As Charles poured two fingers into each glass, John Wilkes said, "… with my history of failures, now that Lee is near collapse, your invitation for this morning surprised me! Did you bring me in for a whipping or to expedite my unfortunate demise?"

Charles chuckled before they drained their glasses. He moved the bottle and glasses to a table beside his desk and said, "Dead actors are too cheap to sell these days… Confederate dollars are more valuable, as a matter of fact!" When Booth didn't respond, Sumner continued, "I need you to expedite a matter for me; I've learned that Lincoln's new Attorney General, Mister Speed, is looking into my lumber business. Should he, and I think 'will' he is more appropriate, bring charges against me for theft of government property, I will lose and go to jail; a monkey could win that case and Speed is no monkey! I think if we return to the first option we considered for Mister Lincoln, Mister Speed's authority will disappear and with it, his case against me."

Booth gestured for another drink before saying, "You called such a plan too dangerous, too subject to failure because of security and God knows what else. That is why you wanted to kidnap Lincoln rather than kill him.…"

Charles interrupted, "… That was then… now we are desperate men with separate, disparate worries. I just told you of mine… a personal dilemma. Yours is national in scope, a southern patriot's worry that his newborn Confederacy is dying on history's operating table. I feel in my heart our first plan can save us both."

Booth asked for and got a refill… three fingers this time. He drank half of it before saying, "We agreed that the security around Lincoln would require such an exercise to be a murder-suicide."

Sumner smiled. "Originally… now, maybe or maybe not!" He held his breath before asking, "Would you consider assassinating Mister Lincoln if I could assure you of escape and a life free of pursuit and persecution?"

Booth took a deep breath. "Perhaps. Remember, I am a southern patriot, not a suicidal maniac." He shook his head to affirm a willingness to listen.

Charles interrupted. "I will set up an appointment for us to meet again soon. That's when I'll share some thinking. I have a man I want you to meet before you decide if you are in or out of an enterprise you are yet to understand."

15

MOSES Prayer Hall, Philadelphia, Pennsylvania
Friday, April 7, 1865, 10AM

Atwater opened the letter with 'Senate Office Building' on the return address first. He glanced through it before saying aloud, "Tom, you ain't gonna believe this! The Lord is movin' in mysterious ways for us again!"

Tom looked up from his fourth cup of coffee. It was one more than usual. He asked, "What's He movin' for us?"

Atwater smiled. "I know you remember me talking about Senator Sumner. He's the one what got them slaves out of our hair. Well, he's inviting me to come see him next Thursday. The invite's to eat dinner with him and some friends at a fancy restaurant. He says I can bring a dedicated to MOSES friend and abolitionist guest if I like... do you want to go?"

"You bet I do! Yes!"

16

Senate Office Building, Washington, DC
Thursday, April 13, 1865, 2PM

Atwater gripped the knob to Charles Sumner's office door but did not turn it. Tom asked, "Why you just standin' there?"

Atwater sighed, "Tom, I need to warn you about the woman on the other side of this door. She's too good lookin' to be real, and that means she's an angel in disguise or a trap Satan set for the godly… men such as you and me."

"Working for Charles Sumner?"

Tom, sometimes you're so dumb I cringe, thought Atwater. "It means don't take a chance on her beguiling you, Tom! Open your head some more… ain't much getting through today."

With that, he opened the door and led Tom inside.

Marilee smiled. Tom gasped and Atwater kicked his friend's ankle before she said, "Mister Coyle, how good to see you again! I'll let the senator know you are here with your friend, Mister, Mister…"

Tom's face reddened and his voice cracked as he blurted, "I'm Tom Killen, ma'am, and I'm proud to acquaint with you!"

As Marilee entered Charles's office, Atwater hissed, "Let me do the talkin! You right on the verge of makin' a fool of yourself... and me, too!"

Marilee held Sumner's private office door open, and Charles' voice boomed through, "Gentlemen, please come in! I've a friend I want you to meet... one of our own!"

Atwater introduced Tom and then froze as Tom gawked at John Wilkes Booth and exclaimed, "He's you!"

Booth shook hands with both men but kept his eyes locked with Atwater's until Charles asked him, "So, what do you think?"

Booth stepped back. He looked Atwater up and down before musing, "Except for matters of hygiene and dress, we could be the same person!"

The senator pointed to three chairs by his desk and said, "Gentlemen, please, join me for a bit of conversation."

Atwater and Tom sat across from Charles and John Wilkes moved the third chair to the desk's end so he could face the other three. When Charles lit a cigar, Atwater saw the wafting smoke as a shield, a sign of strength and perhaps virile contempt for all who oppose him.

Charles set the cigar in his ashtray and said, "Mister Coyle, please tell my friend Mister Booth of your calling, your relationship with the Lord."

Atwater leaned forward, rested his elbows on Sumner's desk and steepled his fingers. In his most educated sounding voice, he said, "Sir, my friend and I are founding members of the abolitionist movement MOSES, and we would be fugitive from the law without the senator's help.. Why? Sir, we freed nineteen darkies from Stafford, Virginia's Callaghan Plantation in 1860 after a bitter fight to remove them from bondage. I use the term 'bitter' because to succeed, events forced us to kill the family head, his son, and several others. We did not choose to kill; we did God's will and to do His will... well... we smote His enemies." Atwater took on his most benevolent smile and whispered, "The senator here transported them from Philadelphia to North Adams, Massachusetts, and a life as free men... women, too!"

Charles applauded twice before Booth bragged about Atwater and Tom. "Gentlemen, you possess the rarest form of personal courage! That is selfless courage and I salute you!"

As Atwater and Tom blushed, Charles added, "As do I, even though personally I repudiate all acts of violence." Sumner then leaned back, closed his eyes, and interlocked his fingers across his stomach. He seemed in deep meditation.

Tom leaned to Atwater and whispered, "What's he doing?"

Atwater hissed, "Hush, Tom. I'll do all the talking!"

As Charles meditated, or slept, John Wilkes said, "Charles wanted me to hear the account from you personally, but he had told me the Callaghan slaves were in North Adams... He calls you heroes and I honor you as heroes as well, Gentlemen!" He then asked, "Am I correct that you suffered losses as you did God's work."

"Four God-fearing soldiers of the cross died so that Tom and I could bring men, women, and children to Philadelphia... the same ex-slaves the senator shipped to North Adams, to jobs and freedom."

Charles opened his eyes and set his cigar in its ashtray and folded his hands on his ink blotter as he said, "... and you're not in violation of any other laws. You haven't committed any other criminal acts."

Atwater smiled as he said, "... so far as we know, Senator, and we love this country! We'd never harm America on account'a God Himself blew life into its nostrils!" Atwater looked for the right words, and wept as he whispered, "Our only higher allegiance is to the Lord God who declared slavery an abomination! The onliest thing I got to say is that if America conflicts with God, we obey Him."

Charles swiveled his chair and looked out the window. He then looked at Atwater and Tom. "Your words and the words in my heart are the same. Some friends and I have learned of a new challenge America faces and we intend to crush the new heretics, the new slavers. We intend to make certain that God's law is the law of the land for all time."

Tom gasped, "Praise Jesus!"

Atwater hissed, "Shut up, Tom," and said, "That's wonderful news, Senator!"

Charles shared his most godly smile as he added, "I mentioned the possibility of dinner and conversation this evening that addresses the new threat to His will. I hope you and Brother Killen can join us at the Knight's House Restaurant in Georgetown at seven... as my guests!"

Atwater blushed, "We'll be proud to join you. Thank you, Sir...

"Christ driven patriots such as you men will help us focus on the godly conclusions this country needs."

Atwater and Tom stood. Charles escorted them to his reception area, shook their hands, and bade them goodbye until that evening.

Sumner returned to his private office door and looked at the still seated John Wilkes Booth. He raised an eyebrow but didn't speak. Booth answered the unspoken question. "I'm in if you can make all the pieces fit."

As they entered the stairwell, Atwater's emotions took control of his mind and body. "We're blessed! God brought us Senator Sumner when we needed him, and I think he wants us to join him in the vanguard of America's Christian soldiers! Tom, for a second time, and if this ain't Archangel stuff, I've seen none, we will fulfill His will!" He whispered, "I think Jesus will do something good for us after this one, too! We proved ourselves again and again!"

Tom took a deep breath before opining a dark fear. "Sometimes, I wonder about how serious the senator takes us. Looked like he was laughing at us some, a little, anyway."

Atwater sneered. "That's crazy, Tom. Don't forget we decided that we're better off with me handling stuff, doin' the thinkin' and talkin'." He chuckled before he added, "Ain't no shame in staying quiet, not getting' in over your head, and rememberin' who Saint Sword is and who he ain't, OK?"

The expression on Tom's face showed doubt, but he nodded his head anyhow.

Atwater continued, "With that settled, we both look nasty, and you smell bad. We need to take a bath and get our clothes cleaned if we gonna look as fancy as them big shots we're to meet and talk to at dinner tonight. They set store by that sort of thing."

"Where we gonna do that?" asked. Tom.

"Washington has one of them English YMCAs. We can clean up and get a little rest there for cheap." Tom blinked his eyes in rapid succession. Atwater knew what that meant. "Tom, I see unease in your face. A United States Senator wouldn't buy dinner for people he didn't have no respect for, would he? Just think about that for a minute!"

From the doorway, Marilee watched Atwater and Tom disappear down the stairs. She asked Senator Sumner. "Shall I tell the others your new friends will join us tonight?"

Charles answered, "Go over to Representatives Edwin Wallace, Lewis Dark, and Ben Singer's offices. Tell them our guests have everything we need to proceed." He added, "One thing more,

Marilee, tell them all to wear their Jesus hats tonight and make sure our military friends do the same. Tell them I don't want anyone running off our True Believers."

17

**Knight's House, Georgetown, Washington, DC
Thursday, April 13, 1865, 7PM**

Atwater tugged at the carriage driver's jacket, and asked, "Is that
the Knight's House? The big white one with all the lanterns?" It
was.

He pointed to the restaurant's veranda and said, "Look, Tom,
yonder's Senator Sumner, two army uniforms, and three rich
women in long dresses; I'll bet those women are with the folks
we're meeting."

The driver pulled to the curb. Atwater paid their fare and
tipped with a flourish because you never know who's watching.
He and Tom stared at the restaurant. As they absorbed its maj-
esty, Tom said, "I feel like I'm going into a church."

Atwater leaned near his friend's ear and whispered, "Tom, just
do what I do and remember that when the serious stuff starts,
you do the keeping quiet and I'll do the talking."

"Are you saying you been in a place like this before? I didn't
know that! Well, no reason for you to worry about me embarrass-
ing either of us! I'm going to eat a big dinner and be nice to all the

big shots and talk about flowers and such with some women! By the way, when were you in a place like this?"

Atwater groaned. "I didn't say I had, Tom. What I said was you do what I do!" Atwater hoped for the best.

Tom said, "Well, while I'm smiling and being nice, maybe one of us can figure out where we'll sleep tonight, since the cash we're already low on ain't ours and we have to replace every dime at the Prayer Hall."

"Me and Jesus have everything in hand. Now it's time for you to hush!" Atwater then called up the stairs, "Senator Sumner, here we are, right on time, as promised!"

While raising both hands in a welcoming gesture, Charles whispered to Marilee, who stood beside him, "Your success will bring you both joy and wealth. If you fail, my fortune will collapse and your life will end in an immediate and painful death. Remember that."

She nodded, whispered, "I won't fail," and then directed a smile at Atwater's face.

Atwater felt the smile; he knew the Devil was working on his mind with her beauty and he forced his gaze to Charles. "Senator Sumner, Tom and I are delighted to join you for dinner tonight." His eyes drifted back to the *kindercoffee* tone of Marilee's face and neck. He hoped he sounded casual as he said, "Miss Lewallen, your presence is an unexpected pleasure for Tom and me. May I say your gown is lovely?"

She smiled. Those white, straight, shiny teeth allowed a glimpse at her beautiful pink tongue, an image that the Devil was using to bait Atwater, make him want to touch it with his own, and he knew it. She answered, "What a lovely thing to say, Mister Coyle. I'm pleased to see you and Mister Killen as well."

Atwater stole the quickest of glances along Marilee's bare

neck and shoulders. Three intertwined gold chains caressed her breasts and drew his eye across her flawless skin as her deeply cut emerald-green gown pushed her breasts toward him, allowed them to call to him, and capture his every thought and dream.

When Tom realized she had rendered his friend mute, he said, "Miss Marilee, Ma'am, Atwater, and I are honored by your presence, and we look forward to a lovely evening."

Charles smiled. It was obvious Marilee's face and breasts had Atwater under complete control and just may convince his new abolitionist friend to do anything Charles asked. He took Marilee's arm and nodded toward the door. "Gentlemen, shall we go inside?"

In the foyer, Marilee leaned near Atwater's ear and her soft breath continued to weaken his resolve as she whispered, "Judge Simon Fincannon is the older man. He will sit on the Senator's left. He likes to preen, but he says nothing to anybody. Representatives Edwin Wallace, Lewis Dark, and Ben Singer are inside somewhere. None of their wives attended this evening. They're sour little women, anyway, so it's no loss."

A smitten Atwater groped for something to say. "Your beauty graces the entire restaurant, Miss Lewallen."

She smiled... those teeth, that pink tongue... and she continued, "The shorter of the two women with me on the veranda is Mrs. Elijah Spoon, the wife of Colonel Elijah Spoon of the Harrisburg Spoons. They made a fortune manufacturing farm implements and since 1860 they've made another one by manufacturing bayonets, knives, and other things for war." She glanced at Charles and continued, "The Senator speaks highly of the Spoon family."

Atwater cared about the Spoon family much less than he cared about Marilee's pushed-up mocha breasts, which the Devil kept right in his face. He closed his eyes and shivered as he answered Marilee, "We see their dedication to the Union in the products they make."

She batted her eyes at him and briefly took his hand. "As do I…"

The *maître d'hôtel* appeared and exchanged quick whispers with the Charles before scurrying across the room and through the kitchen doors. Seated between Atwater and Tom, Marailee thought, *"I ache for these fools, especially since they freed some of my ethnic kin".* She sighed and added, "… *but I'd better worry about myself, first. I've been warned."*

Tom muttered under his breath, "Look at all of them forks!"

Marilee heard Tom. She tried to help both men relax by brushing her fingers along both Atwater's and Tom's sleeves. She smiled while whispering, "Gentlemen, as a little girl, I once dined with two handsome and gallant men, and tonight I do it again. Unlike most *déjà vu* moments, this one is my good fortune."

Her sweet words, her smile, and those glorious breasts continued to beguile Atwater. Like no one he'd ever known, this woman at once was worldly, a friend, a child, a fluttering pixie, and a seductress. He knew her attention would go elsewhere if he didn't answer. "Where did you spend your childhood, Miss Lewallen?"

"I was born in Haiti. I am light-skinned because my father was French and my mother a mulatto girl, the unintended daughter of a European sailor and my grandmother." She looked away and smiled wistfully while adding, "I never knew my grandmother, but my mother was beautiful. I keep a drawing of her at the office. I'll show it to you some day. You'll see what I mean when I say beautiful…"

Not wanting to be left out of the conversation, Tom asked, "If you don't mind me asking, what of your father?"

After the Waiters opened the table and placed four more chairs, she continued, "Mama was the French *Liaison d'état*'s mistress in Port-au-Prince. He paid the convent to raise me, and the nuns taught me manners, mathematics, and to read and write French, English, Creole, and German. As time passed and the Liaison aged, the money slowed down and then stopped. That was when he sold mother and me on the slave traders' block. A Florida family, friends of the Senator and Mrs. Sumner, bought both of us when I was eleven. Thankfully, the Liaison insisted we stay together."

After a peek down the front of Marilee's dress, Atwater whispered, "Wow!"

"Mother's still with them in Florida. When I turned fourteen, my master's wife decided I distracted her husband and sons and insisted that the master sell me. The Senator bought me, freed me, and gave me a job with his wife. Now I work in his office; end of story!"

After more of a gulp than a swallow, Atwater said, "... speaks well for him."

Charles smiled at Marilee. She smiled in reply before folding her hands in her lap and nodding to Mrs. Spoon, who steered a conversation to her family's contribution to the war effort. As she spoke, Marilee touched Atwater and Tom's hands and whispered, "Colonel Spoon will resign from the service and return to Harrisburg soon. Mrs. Spoon brought some manservants to pack his things."

Atwater asked, "You mentioned the judge and the others, but who is the old general with the muttonchops?" As an afterthought, he added, "Nice of him to bring his daughter..."

"The general is Lemuel Arthur Clarkhorn. He's military attaché and adjunct officer to Attorney General James Speed. Mrs.

Clarkhorn is his dinner companion."

Tom snickered. "I can tell you two things about him. He's got money, and he's lucky!"

"She is the third Mrs. Clarkhorn," added Marilee.

"What does the General do for the Attorney General?"

"He provides needed information concerning either Congress or upstate New York and alters misdirected policies before they become law. He also provides control where it's missing in several ways." She leaned close enough for Atwater to smell her perfume, which was delicate. It smelled expensive, and he liked it. He dared to touch her hand. She gently pulled it away and whispered, "Later..." She glanced around the table before adding, "Returning to the General for a moment, never forget that he habitually punishes those who oppose him, both in and out of government."

"Ain't he too public to do stuff like that?" wondered Atwater.

"Colonel Spoon defends the General, and the General defends the Spoon family's government contracts. The arrangement is what my Nuns called '*Quid pro quo*'."

After a moment's thought, Atwater asked, "I don't know what that means. Are you saying Clarkhorn's the biggest dog in the bone yard except for the Senator and that Spoon gets dirty for him?"

Marilee smiled...

Charles crooked a finger toward the *maître d'hôtel* and he raced to the senator's side. In a voice just loud enough for the others to hear, Charles said, "Humphrey, send the bill for this to my office and add twenty percent for the staff if they do us right this evening. Remember, none of the Devil's grape will shame our table as we worship our Lord and his bounty."

With a soft smile, Humphrey answered, "As usual, Sir."

"We'll have some of your gourmet dark coffee and I'd like you to serve the ladies and our special guests, Mister Coyle and Mister Killen, the gentlemen on either side of Miss Marilee, in your gold-inlay cups. The usual tall green ones will be fine for the rest of us."

Honored almost beyond description, Atwater said, "Senator, Tom and I don't expect..."

Charles interrupted, "... Mr. Coyle, it pleases us to pay you tribute in this small way."

Atwater gestured to include Tom in his answer as he said, "We're only His tool. We're nothing more than His instrument."

A murmur of approval circled the table as the waiters distributed the gold inlayed special cups and poured steaming coffee into each. Humphrey then brought Bourbon filled tall opaque green glasses to the table without comment. Charles tasted his and said, "Amen, Humphrey!"

Amens resounded around the table and drew a few stares from other tables. The senator smiled benevolently and whispered, "Gentlemen, your role as the Lord's instrument rings true on this night of nights. I say that because the Lord has again called us to his service. While in prayer, he told me to step beyond abolition, to save the republic from a satanic man who would sully, indeed destroy, it!"

Tom added, "I say Amen without knowin' no details!"

Sumner whispered, "I'll share the details of our charge after dinner, Brother Tom; some of it this evening and the rest tomorrow! Soon, everything will be very clear to you and Brother Atwater."

After a soft 'Amen', Atwater thought 'tonight and tomorrow!' before looking around the table. Like Tom, the placement, the sheer amount of silverware that surrounded each plate, confused him. It was a dilemma he resolved by choosing his biggest fork and eating a dinner fit for a European King. Afterward, over an airy fruit pastry, Elijah Spoon said, "Senator, as I know every detail of what lies ahead and Mrs. Spoon is exhausted, we must bid all a fond *adieu*."

Charles already knew. He answered, "No apology is necessary, Colonel. I know delicate ladies need their beauty rest, especially those as lovely as Mrs. Spoon! I trust you can meet us tomorrow morning..."

Elijah stood. He assisted his wife to her feet, and they said their goodnights. Outside, she whispered, "I shudder to think how the old fool's black girl is involved in this."

Elijah whispered, "Moral support, my dear; she provides the senator moral support and does so with great vigor."

Darleen poked his ribs and laughed. "She may boost Charles' morale, but I doubt if our definitions of the moral support she offers are similar, much less identical."

Elijah chuckled under his breath.

Darlene continued, "I fear she uses that great vigor in other ways."

18

**Knight's House, Georgetown, Washington, DC
Thursday, April 13, 1865, 8:45PM**

Once the wagon rolls downhill...

The embellished accounts of MOSES's efforts to free slaves that Atwater recited embarrassed Tom, although he agreed with his friend's concluding offer. "We'll be proud to help in any new battle with Satan and his demons!"

Atwater and Tom accepted and enjoyed a series of accolades from the politicians, the ladies, and General Clarkhorn until the dining room was empty save their table. One of the exhausted waiters and cooks, all gathered around a table by the kitchen door, made eye contact with Charles.

The Senator called Humphrey over. "Tell your staff that their excellent service had earned everyone a big tip. And then go to the hotel side and get two rooms, one for each of my guests, fully stocked with toiletries. They'll be here two nights. Add their room charges to this bill." Nodding toward the staff, he added, "Send them home. You're to sit up front in case we need something from the kitchen over the next while. We won't keep you awake too long."

With Humphry gone, Marilee held her breath as Charles said, "Now, let's get to the matter's core." He concentrated his gaze on Atwater and Tom. "As I am sure you already know, Brother Coyle, Armageddon is at hand. In prayer, Archangel Gabriel told me, and I know he told you earlier, that unknown to patriots, the Devil has supported not only the Southern states. Indeed, he also supported some of our great nation's leaders, who soon will expose their treasonous mutual allegiance. I regret to add that the President of the United States, Abraham Lincoln, is among them!"

Atwater knew not to say he'd had no such conversation. He nodded and whispered to Tom in a voice loud enough for the others to hear. "I was told not to say anything Tom, not even to you. I followed orders. I didn't have a choice."

Charles continued, "Now, at war's end, all may have been for naught. Slavery is about to be reborn and only a righteous few stand against it and with God."

General Clarkhorn interjected, "God provided strength to the Spartans at Thermopylae! Although we stand fewer than their three hundred, His sword and shield will protect us."

Tom looked awestruck as he blurted, "I can't see Lincoln bein' no slaver..."

Atwater, afraid his friend would ruin the evening, and the praise he was enjoying, hushed Tom with, "Of course I know all about this and while I praise Jesus's sword and shield, I don't know nothin' about no Spartans neither..."

Charles feared the General had distracted Atwater and Tom, so he said, "That's an old soldiering story, Brother Coyle. It's an account of victory when outnumbered. As for matters at hand..." He paused, looked around the table. Atwater and Tom were with him again, so he continued, "Satan has justified slaving to everybody at the top of our government. I'm talking about Lincoln, the Vice-President, too, along with Generals Meade and Grant and the rest of them. Now, they may not know somebody's controlling them. Ol' Billy is clever, more clever than wise, and God said we're to act against him." After a pause and a sigh, he added, "We're to cleanse evil from His chosen nation. That includes making sure all men are and will remain free."

The senator's powerful words, carefully planned for Atwater and Tom, worked. Atwater asked, "Praise Jesus, but how are we going to do something like that?"

Charles leaned near Atwater and confided in a soft voice, "The process is simple. If ill befalls Satan, who now controls Abraham Lincoln's mind and body, the Vice-President's mind and body, and the Speaker-of-the-House's all at once, I will accept the mantle as President in His name. All the good things will remain. The slaving will not."

Confusion danced on Tom's face as he muttered. "It sounds like you're talking about killing Lincoln, the rest of 'em, too."

"We're not after Lincoln or any other human being. We're after Satan and if we have to go through Lincoln or anybody else to be tools for Jesus' divine retribution, we have no choice. My brothers, The Lord chose you because you smote Satan's slaveholders at the Callaghan Plantation! You did that in His name and God told me that the Republic needs you to do it again; this time for everybody."

Atwater twitched as Tom whispered, "I... I mean..."

"Others among us will remove Vice-President Johnson and the rest. You Christian Soldiers are to strip victory from Satan once we force him from Abraham Lincoln's mortal shell in an act that is not murder. Indeed, Lincoln's soul is in heaven as we speak.

Gabriel says you are to lead the soldiers and police away from the man pulling the Devil from Lincoln's shell. With you, Gentlemen, we shall restore God's supremacy and free His children."

Tom sipped his coffee and said, "Atwater's in charge of us, but I need to pray on it…"

Atwater sensed Tom's uneasy emotions. He tried to calm his friend. "The Lord works in mysterious ways. If He offers this path to redeem our godly nation, who are we to doubt Him?"

"It sounds crazy," said Tom. "I want to do God's will, but this don't sound like killing to free darkies to me. I ain't never even thought about Satan taking hold of President Lincoln."

Charles shrugged his shoulders as he answered, "The call is from God and Gabriel, not me." He selected his next words with care. "If you choose not to help, others will fight for the Lord, will answer His call."

Atwater was in. "If you wind up president, who'll swear you in? As a man of the cloth, I'd…"

Charles beamed a smile and answered, "Saint Sword, if you would so honor me…"

Atwater enjoyed thinking of how his name would look in the newspapers. He decided the inauguration would be a good place to finish his transition to Saint Sword. "Exactly what we gonna do tricking the soldiers…?"

"We'll go over this tomorrow, but for now, I can say that the Lord wants you and Tom as misleaders, distractions. Some may call you straw men. In fact, those are the exact words Gabriel used when he talked about what he wanted from you and Tom. If I didn't have other duties, I'd proudly join you as you wear His mantle and distract Satan."

The reasoning behind their call to duty cleared for Tom; he exclaimed, "If Gabriel said it, I believe it! Since Atwater knew something was going on, that's more proof he's 'Saint Sword'! I gotta add, though, the only straw man I ever saw stands in a cornfield!"

Atwater struggled to be benevolent. He said, "It's all going to be fine, clear as a bell, Tom. All we do now is listen."

Charles touched Atwater's forearm and said, "God will provide some last thoughts tomorrow morning. In the meantime, Miss Lewallen has additional information to share with you in private." He glanced at Tom. "Until tomorrow, Brother Killen." He then looked at Marilee and added, "Do you mind addressing these last issues and the attire Jesus chose for him to wear tomorrow evening with Minister Coyle? May I suggest in your quarters? I fear prying eyes and ears are everywhere."

With a nod and a smile, Marilee leaned forward to sip from a glass of water. As she did so, her neckline fell from her body, which allowed Atwater a bug-eyed leer down the front of her dress. He thought, *Lordamighty! I can see halfway to Mexico!* She sat up and sipped her water again before smiling directly at him. Her smile was soft, beautiful, and it framed her snow-white teeth and a tantalizing hint of pink tongue as her eyes penetrated Atwater's soul. In an angelic voice, she answered, "I'm in 114 Minister Coyle; it's on the right at the end of the hall."

Looking at the key Humphry left for him, Atwater said, "I'm 112; looks like we're neighbors!"

Tom looked at his key as well. "201... I'm up on the second floor."

The Senator joyfully slapped the table. "Those are splendid rooms, well chosen by Humphrey! Now, this evening, if you see any soldiers outside, they are Colonel Spoon's men serving as the Lord's lookouts. They'll protect us from any godless interlopers.

Tom's mind flashed from Atwater in Marilee's room... alone... to Abraham Lincoln's Satan occupied body turning on Jesus. It then darted to the certainty that Jesus would tell him everything he needed to know. He asked, "What time you want to get started tomorrow?"

Senator Sumner answered, "General Clarkhorn and I usually eat breakfast at seven, Tom. Join us then for a little private talk." He turned to Atwater. "Brother Coyle, if you'll join us at nine. Tomorrow will be a long day for us, but we are Christian soldiers preparing to do God's will."

General Clarkhorn ran a finger through his muttonchops. He said, "...' I might add my role tomorrow morning will be to assist the senator as he requests, nothing more. He is our Oracle! The three stars on my tunic are only my earthly symbol of our holy cause." Turning to Atwater, he added, "Brother Coyle, will you lead us in prayer?"

19

**Knight's House Whiskey Room, Georgetown,
Washington, DC
Thursday, April 13, 1865, 10PM**

Charles Sumner watched General Clarkhorn enter through the swinging door. After gesturing to the General, he called for two Bourbons, neat, and bade Lemuel to join him. When their drinks were in hand and they were alone, he asked, "Are we ready?"

The General answered, "We are indeed. Booth will make his move at Ford Theater at around 10:45. He knows 'Our American Cousin' well. A funny scene, one that always draws laughs, will occur about then and amid the laughter he will kill Lincoln. He plans to leap from the Presidential Box to the stage, it's only eight feet, and exit through the rear door while everyone is still wondering if he was part of the play."

Two horses and a friend of his named David Herold will be at the rear door. They will join us here posthaste where Herold will exchange identities with Brother Killen on the second floor and Booth will exchange clothes with Coyle, who will be in Marilee's quarters. Behind the hotel, Coyle will take John Wilkes' mount and Killen will take Herold's. They will ride south, cross the Potomac, to Port Royal, Virginia, which is a desolate and rural area." After a smile, he added, "You know the rest."

"Colonel Spoon, his men, and I will be right behind them, and that means that the saga of Abraham Lincoln and John Wilkes Booth will end as suddenly as it began! Your gold mine of a lumber mill, my percentage of its profits, and my share of Elijah Spoon's ongoing no-bid Government contracts will continue for the foreseeable future!" He paused. "They will grow handsomely when you assume the Presidency in what, three to six months?"

"God willing, fewer than three!"

"And after that, what title will you choose? Will you be Emperor of North America or King Charles I? And how quickly will you do so and enrich me more? Three months, six?"

With a victor's smile, Sumner answered, "Today I think King. Emperor sounds a little affected to my ears..."

Lemuel chortled before turning serious again. "The only spoiler could be Killen. His challenge of our Lincoln-Satan link made me uneasy."

Charles no longer questioned Tom's devotion. He explained, "Killen is in... I think he's a little worried about Coyle and Marilee, but he believed me when I told him to go to bed because Atwater and Miss Lewallen, as he called her, would share a late-night prayer service with my wife. As for Coyle, Marilee, in all her glory, is probably on him right now. If so, and I assure you she is, he will do anything she says, no questions asked."

Clarkhorn snickered, "She must have magic in that thing!"

A knowing Charles smiled. "I guarantee it!"

20

**Knight's House, Room 114, Georgetown, Washington, DC
Thursday, April 13, 1865, 10:05PM**

Riding faster and faster...

Atwater slicked his hair down and cracked his knuckles at Marilee's door. He prayed "Lord, don't let the Devil work his way into me while I'm in a lady's room tonight." He then tapped, waited five seconds, and whispered, "Miss Marilee, it's Atwater. Do you still want to talk to me tonight?"

Marilee's voice was soft, melodic, as she answered, "Give me one minute! I'll be right with you, Minister Coyle."

He sensed temptation, feared it was at hand, but even Jesus would have trouble making him back away now. He felt lust in his heart. It bothered him.

When Marilee opened the door, all Atwater could do was gasp. She wore a diaphanous bright white nightgown that barely touched her thighs, long diamond encrusted silver earrings, and nothing else. She smiled. It was that delicious smile. Her luscious blue eyes climbed inside his heart as she spun slowly and asked, "Do you like my new nightgown? It's the latest thing from Paris and it's so comfortable!" She touched his hand to her hip. "It's so soft. Can you tell?"

Was the fabric soft? Atwater did not know, but he grunted, "Uh-huh! Soft!" as he spied a small mole, a beauty mark, below and to the left of her navel. He could see it and everything else under that nightgown, everything! Bright red and trembling, he forced himself to say, "I… uh… I think maybe I'm intruding on your bedtime… keeping you from gettin' your sleep."

She walked to the bed, sat down, and leaned back, resting her weight on her hands. She allowed her bare feet to drift back and forth, as though a sensual stream toyed with them. Saint Sword took a deep breath as he counted ten perfectly pedicured tan and pink toes.

After Marilee patted the mattress beside her and asked Atwater to sit, he went to the straight-backed chair near the front door, sat, and folded his arms. With a smile as much little girl as vamp, she stood and walked to her closet. Her hips made him think of tropical islands and exotic women as she cooed over her shoulder, "This won't take long. I just want to show you what you'll wear tomorrow night… your 'straw man' outfit…" She removed a blousy-sleeved white silk shirt, a pair of brown wool-silk blend trousers, and a pair of highly polished brown shoes from her closet. After placing the shoes at his feet and laying the shirt and trousers across her left arm, she continued, "The fit must be perfect. We can't afford any mistakes." Confused, he looked around the room before Marilee added, "You may change behind my dressing screen, if you wish." When he didn't move, she again gave him that smile while adding, "I won't peek."

The floor creaked as Atwater carried the clothes and shoes behind the screen. He glanced around it and blushed again when he saw Marilee had returned to her bed and somehow her nightgown had slipped off her left shoulder. His voice quivered as he said, "I'll be out in a minute."

As Atwater walked from behind the screen, Marilee sat up and her nightgown slipped lower, which exposed more of her left breast. He gasped.

Innocent sensuality, a coy promise, filled her voice as Marilee whispered, "Come here so I can examine the fit..." He did so, and she aroused him with gentle tugs and smoothing wipes across his new clothes.

With nature in charge of his body, Atwater looked down and feared she knew the effect she had on him. His face became a vivid crimson, and he stammered, "Miss Marilee, I know I shouldn't be lookin' but your left bosom, except the working' part, is right in front of me."

She slipped her hands across the front of his trousers while whispering, "I feel strength. I feel your power, your manliness. I feel it in my heart as much as I do in my hands." She unbuttoned his shirt and cooed, "Saint Sword, God wants me to please you tonight and to make certain you rest, sleep well, afterward. He told me to have you rested, vigorous, and prepared for tomorrow."

Atwater neither stuttered nor stammered, but his voice cracked once as he said, "Miss Marilee... This ain't personal, but the Devil himself is after me all the time, tempting me and..."

She slipped his shirt free, folded it, and laid it on the chair beside her bed. After undoing his trousers' top button, she removed her nightgown and laid it atop Atwater's shirt.

Her clear blue eyes glistened. Atwater's heart nestled into them as she traced a finger down his arm and asked, "Do you think I'm of the Devil, Atwater? I assure you. I'm not."

He folded his arms and tapped a foot. "Oh, no, ma'am... I don't... but, well, I know Satan is tricky."

He forced his eyes away from hers. Marilee responded by kissing his belly and asking, "Atwater, have you, have you ever known a woman before…? Biblically known, I mean."

The question both embarrassed Atwater and made him proud. He answered, "No, ma'am. I took a vow like them Catholic fellows do, so, no ma'am, I ain't."

Her tongue flicked around his navel as she asked, "Do you believe me when I say I am of God and not Satan? Do you believe I want both of us to do God's will?"

His voice quaked, almost broke, as he answered, "I say yes to both of them questions. I believe you."

Marilee removed his pants, laid them over his shirt and her nightgown, and pulled his shoulders to the bed. "You will work hard tomorrow. A 'straw man's' job never is easy. That will be tomorrow, not tonight. Tonight, God wants me to replenish your body and assuage your soul."

21

**Knight's House, Room 114, Georgetown,
Washington, DC
Friday, April 14, 1865, 9:30PM**

Almost twenty-four hours later, sweat-soaked and gasping for breath, Atwater rolled onto his left side so he could touch Marilee and talk to her perfect face. He said, "I got to say, God rewarded me with something wonderful last night, something I want you and me to do all day every day, c'ept for right now. Right now, I don't think I can!"

She pecked a brief kiss on his lips…

Atwater committed himself. "Marilee, I love you even though you are a quarter darky. It doesn't matter to me; I love you! Will you marry me, be my wife, my co-minister? You know, darkies come to the Prayer Hall, too! I think they'd enjoy hearing you talk even more than me."

She demurred behind a sweet smile. "Such a serious question! I need to think about it. Will you ask me again after you finish your duties? I need a week to consider such a privilege."

He blushed. "Yes'm, and between now and then I don't think

Tom or any of them local or army fellows need to know that we might nuptualize. No sense in havin' them or their wives getting het up, planning a wedding, until you give me the answer I want to hear."

22

**Our American Cousin at the Ford Theater,
Washington, DC
Friday, April 14, 1865, 10:45PM**

Raucous laughter filled the theater below as John Wilkes Booth touched his Derringer pistol behind and above Abraham Lincoln's left ear. When he pulled the trigger, Mary Todd Lincoln and their guests, Major Henry Rathbone, and his fiancée Clara Harris, reacted with shock and Rathbone reached for Booth. He failed as the assassin leaped to the stage. Some in the audience continued to titter and laugh. They thought the hysteria, and the leap, were part of the play. Most understood what had happened the instant Booth shouted, "Sic semper tyrannis! The South is avenged," and half-limped, half- ran backstage and out the rear door.

A short, thin man who lacked his companion's physical and intelligence gifts, David Herold watched Booth pull himself into his saddle. When Booth urged his horse to run, David pulled his reins left and hissed, "Let's get the Hell out of here!"

23

**Knight's House, Room 114, Georgetown, Washington, DC
Friday, April 14, 1865, 11:05PM**

Atwater admired his image in Marilee's full-length mirror. He turned a complete circle, craned his neck to see every angle, and then looked into her eyes.

Marilee smiled...

Atwater knew she controlled his every mortal fiber, and he loved her. No woman had ever done for him what she did, and he knew she was the only one that could. He asked, "Do I look right? Tell me the truth."

She tilted her head, exposed her beautiful neck. "You are the most handsome man in the entire world, and I love you! You are perfect! You look more like Booth than Booth looks like himself and..." She touched her right index finger to his nose.

"... And what?"

"... And you have a good soul. We'll both be happy when I answer your question." She read Atwater's face. "Why don't you smile? Have you changed your mind about me?"

"Lord, no! I'm happier to hear that than I can say! It's just I have a lot tumbling through my mind right now, startin' with what Tom said about Lincoln and him not likin' slavery at dinner. I mean, I love Jesus, but I hope this ain't a mistake, as big a one as I can imagine..."

She walked to him, tucked a pouch with twenty dollars in gold inside in his pocket, and pressed her lips to his while bringing one of his hands to her breast. She whispered, "But Lincoln did and still does, my Saint... and we know it! That's why God called us! We will avenge a horrible sin in His name. God trusts us, and we are right because God is right!"

Her words and eyes convinced Atwater. "I guess I needed to hear you say it."

Three quick raps sounded at Marilee's door. She opened it and John Wilkes Booth limped inside. He closed the door. She gasped, "Your leg! You're in pain! What happened?"

"I think I broke it jumping onto that damnable stage; my foot twisted under me when I landed, and I heard something snap. It hurts like Hell!"

"This could ruin everything! You being unable to walk, much less run, isn't something the senator even considered! A limp will draw every eye, make people remember and think of you, and that won't do!" Marilee continued in a fast stammer. "A doctor... I don't know... let me think! The hotel must have access to one..."

"Am I supposed to go now?" asked Atwater.

Marilee answered, "Yes, my darling, your horse is behind the hotel. Do you know what you and Tom are to do and where you are to go... no doubts at all?"

Coyle and Booth locked eyes before Atwater could answer. They said, "Amazing!" in unison before Atwater answered, "Me and Tom hide out of sight for a while, let 'em get all fanned out, and it'll be easier for us to cross the Potomac to Port Royal on the twenty-second or twenty-third. A boat to somewhere safe will pick us up there." His voice trembled. "I... uh... I'll send word when I can... we can finish talking about the future of us then..."

She kissed his cheek again. "Go with God!"

As Atwater ran down the hall, Booth closed the door and laughed, "Go with God, my ass!"

Outside, Atwater hurried to the rear of the Knight's House. Tom, already mounted, brought Atwater his horse. In a single, almost choreographed movement, they dug their heels into the horses' sides and growled, "Let's ride!"

24

**Knight's House, Room 114, Georgetown,
Washington, DC
Friday, April 14, 1865, 11:30PM**

Marilee stepped behind her dressing screen and put on an aging and frumpy housecoat. She pulled it tight, returned to Booth, and said, "Change into Atwater's old clothes before I send for the hotel doctor."

John Wilkes did so. As he changed, he smelled the shirt's sleeve and laughed through his pain. "This is the cheapest, ugliest, and most foul-smelling garment ever to touch my body!" He smiled as he added, "… and even more foul, you addressed him in such endearing terms! What a wonderful employee you are!"

Marilee blotted a tear from her eye before she sneered, "Shut up, you crazy pig! I just sent a decent man to die for you, for your lousy ass!"

Booth chuckled, "Indeed you did, my dear; indeed, you did, and my good fellow David and I appreciate it! As we lie in the sun on Rio's beaches amid beautiful women, we will pray for Coyle, or should we refer to him as Saint Sword? We want him to receive the benefit."

25

Battery Kemble Park, Washington, DC
Sunday, April 23, 1865, 8AM

General Lemuel Clarkhorn kept a watchful eye as Colonel Elijah Spoon addressed his troops, "Gentlemen, today we shall redeem the reputation of the Republic! General Clarkhorn just advised me we now know where we will find the assassin, John Wilkes Booth and his accomplice, a man yet unknown. Under General Clarkhorn's personal leadership, we will pursue them, capture them, and bring them to justice. Further, I allow any man to use deadly force against either Booth or his companion should he feel endangered, or should he see a fellow soldier endangered. Anybody have a question?"

There were no questions, but a lot of eager sounds. Clarkhorn nodded to Spoon, who made an identical gesture to his Sergeant Major. They rode south.

26

**Bank of the Rappahannock River, near
Port Royal, Virginia
Sunday, April 23, 1865, 4:30PM**

After nine days of running and hiding in fear, Atwater looked over the Rappahannock River and groaned. "First no boat on the Potomac, now no boat here! This ain't right, Tom. I think the devil done struck back at us!"

Tom answered, "I think it's too soon to be the devil's work. He's smart, but he ain't that smart!" After they walked their horses to the water's edge, he drew some conclusions. "Things can go wrong. We both know that, and if it's too soon to think about Ol' Billy's hijinks, maybe it's just bad luck. Let's give our luck some time to change by hiding and thinking how we can get across this river... that other bank was Reb country, and they ain't likely to know about Lincoln since they don't get mail anymore. I doubt they get newspapers, either."

As Tom waited for Atwater to respond, fate intervened in the person of William S. Jett, a former soldier in the 9th Virginia Cavalry. Tom amazed Atwater, who went along with the ruse, when he told Jett his name was David Herold, and his companion was James W. Boyd... two ex-Rebs trying to make their way home from Petersburg. Jett, a disillusioned southern patriot, agreed to take them across the river the next day.

27

Richard H. Garrett Farm, Port Royal, Virginia
Monday, April 24, 1865, 6:50PM

A single step led to the Garrett family's front porch, where William Jett stopped his horse the next afternoon. Atwater and Tom did the same. Jett introduced them as ex-rebels, Boyd, and Herold, and the Garretts agreed to shelter them. That night Atwater and Tom slept well.

28

Richard H. Garrett Farm, Port Royal, Virginia
Wednesday, April 26, 1865, 1:30AM

Until you hit the tree stump...

The sound of clopping hooves, a lot of them, awakened Atwater from a sound sleep. He looked outside, saw General Lemuel Clarkhorn, Colonel Elijah Spoon, and at least a hundred troops on horseback. He awakened Tom. "Something ain't right outside! I see that General Clarkhorn, and the Spoon Colonel, too. A bunch of troopers on horseback are with them. I think they're after us!"

Tom wiped his eyes and squinted outside through a lower corner of their bedroom window before he said, "For what... they said they were on Jesus' side, like us."

"Well... I say we think more about that while we get our guns and hightail it out of here!" He finished buttoning his pants and his shirt while looking out the back door. He saw no soldiers and a line of trees that led to the tobacco barn.

Tom looked over Atwater's shoulder. "Let's get over there while we can. They ain't likely to go into a smoky place like that and when they go on, we can get into the woods and go in the opposite direction! I can't believe they're doin' this! How'd they find us, anyway?"

Afraid to ask himself the same question, Atwater answered, "Don't matter... let's run."

After making their way to the tobacco barn, Atwater reassured Tom, "This government ain't nothing compared to the Kingdom of Heaven and we're on official business for Jesus. That means we'll not stand down unless Jesus tells us that's what he wants. I think it's more likely He'll kick their fannies all the way back to Washington!"

Atwater heard voices outside. He peeked through a cracked plank. The Garretts, all of them, were talking to General Clarkhorn and pointing in different directions. When the general jerked a thumb toward a wagon behind his troops, they walked in that direction.

Lemuel Clarkhorn and Elijah Spoon scanned the area with their telescopes from horseback. Soon, Clarkhorn whispered, "If those nitwits still think they're doing God's will, and that's likely, they won't surrender. Tell your men to surround the farm; create a circle. Tell them to shrink the circle until the fools show themselves."

Ten minutes later, as men talked behind and beside the barn, Atwater whispered, "We gotta change tactics, Tom." He shouted through the front door. "Whose evil is this? Is it yours, Clarkhorn? Jesus knows you are betraying him, and He commands you to stop, to repent!" Leaning near Tom again, he continued, "Satan's done tricked us but we ain't finished! Ol' Billy knows them strutting around out there ain't nothing beside Jesus! All we must do is praise His name and he'll get us out of this mess!"

Suddenly, Tom fired two shots through the partly opened barn door and shouted, "Praise His Holy name! Out you Demons!"

Atwater fired twice before screaming, "The flesh trader is dead, praise Jesus!"

Thirty seconds later, General Clarkhorn called toward the tobacco barn, "Surrender or die, Booth... you and your friend! If you come out now, you will live to stand trial! If you don't, we will bring you out dead!"

"I think the Lord should have intervened by now," said Tom. Frightened, he asked, "Atwater... you reckon Jesus wants us to stand trial? You know, tell His story about Lincoln and the slavin' and all."

Atwater loved Tom, whose stupidity appalled him. "Tom, let me ask you again, which of us does the thinkin' and which of us does the listenin' and doin'?"

Tom reflected before he answered. "Usually you, but not this time." He ran through the front door with his hands over his head, shouting, "Don't shoot me! I'm MOSES and I do God and Jesus' will!" Halfway between the barn and the General, he dropped to his knees and begged, "I ain't against nobody! I'm for Jesus! Don't shoot me! Just tell me what you want me to do!"

Frustrated and disappointed, Elijah Spoon shouted, "Face down and shut up, Harald! One more word and I'll shoot you myself!" Turning to a Sergeant, he added, "That is Booth's accomplice, David Harald! Stick a rag in his mouth to keep him quiet. Hog Tie him and lay his ass across a saddle to keep him under control while we transport him to Washington." He then rode to Clarkhorn's side and whispered, "The son of a bitch surrendered! We can't shoot a man that came out with his hands over his head in front of a hundred troopers and the Garretts!"

The obvious answer came to Clarkhorn. "Keep that rag in his mouth! Hell, tie on another one! If it comes out that he isn't Harald, the whole thing will unravel like a ball of twine. Bind the hog-tied son-of-a-bitch across a saddle with his feet and neck strapped together under the horse's belly."

As two soldiers bound him, a struggling Tom tried to shout through his gags, "This is crazy! I told you I ain't done nothin, and I gave up!" He cast his eyes skyward. "Jesus, please help me!" Only Atwater understood Tom's words.

The General asked, "Elijah, who is your most angry man?"

Elijah answered, "Sergeant Corbett, Sergeant Boston Corbett, Sir. He's a crack shot, but he pushes the book to the limit. The man's a thorn in my side, albeit a sometimes useful one! He's a loose cannon, so to speak!"

"That is the man I want. Bring him to me."

In a matter of minutes, Clarkhorn dismissed Spoon and told the Sergeant, "President Lincoln's assassin is in that tobacco barn. His name is John Wilkes Booth."

Corbett's response was as much a question as an answer. "Yes, Sir?"

Clarkhorn answered in a soft, confident voice. "When I say, you are to shoot and kill Booth. You will do so and say you feared for your life. You will not say a word more."

"Understood, Sir."

"I don't want to waste the taxpayer's money putting guilty scum on trial. I want the son of a bitch dead and I hear you are an excellent shot; a man that can handle a weapon."

"I'm happy to follow the General's orders, but are you aware I get in trouble from time to time, Sir? I don't want to project a poor image of your leadership, Sir."

"I am aware of your reputation, and mine is secure. Sergeant, I am prepared to make you a wealthy man after you perform a duty."

"Sir...?"

Clarkhorn kept his voice low and confident. "After you kill the assassin, the army will give you a fast dishonorable discharge, one without a hearing."

"I will, Sir, but tell me, what's dishonorable about killing a presidential assassin?"

"Not a damned thing! What you are doing is exercising a trade. Your failure to contest your dishonorable discharge will bring you wealth beyond your wildest dreams. If you go and remain silent, and do nothing other than what I say, a month from today, a courier will deliver a box to your home. In it, you will find more untraceable money than you can imagine, enough to live the rest of your life in luxury. Another will arrive a year from that day, provided you remain silent and tell no one, not even your wife, about me or our conversation today." His voice took on a hard edge. "The dark side of it all is this: If you talk, you and your wife will die. Do you understand, Sergeant?"

"Two boxes a year apart..."

"Three, if you perform as required... three a year apart. My question was 'do you understand, Sergeant?'"

"I do, Sir. Thank you, Sir. I'm ready to proceed when you say."

"Be ready when I call you, Sergeant. You are dismissed," said Clarkhorn. As Corbett left, the general called for Colonel Spoon. He advised Elijah of his plans. Spoon, ever the good soldier and capitalist, said, "Excellent thinking, Sir!"

29

**Garrett Farm Tobacco Barn, Port Royal, Virginia
Wednesday, April 26, 1865, 5AM**

And stop right there...

Lemuel Clarkhorn called for Colonel Spoon when his pocket watch marked five. "Elijah, torch the barn and tell Corbett to act when the assassin appears."

Spoon's voice showed no emotion. "We will burn his ass out and Corbett will do as ordered, Sir."

"See to it, Colonel."

30

Garrett Farm Tobacco Barn, Port Royal, Virginia
Wednesday, April 26, 1865, 5:10AM

Four flaming torches lay on the tobacco barn's roof over his head and three leaned against the side and rear walls, as Atwater prayed, "Jesus, help me! I don't understand your mysterious ways, but me burning to death in a place like this can't be what you had in mind! Can I surrender and tell them soldiers who I am and who I ain't. I need a sign."

A burning overhead joist separated from the roof, fell, landed near Atwater, and broke apart. On the hard dirt floor, its flames took the shape of an angel's wings.

Atwater knew a sign when he saw one. The Lord wanted him out of the fire and the only way he could do that was to surrender. He pushed the now burning barn door open, raised both hands with his revolver held high to show he wouldn't shoot, and stepped outside.

Sergeant Boston Corbett shot him through the neck. The slug was a big one; it shattered three vertebrae and severed part of Atwater's spinal cord. Atwater collapsed paralyzed from the neck down. His blood pooled on the ground.

<h1 style="text-align:center">31</h1>

Garrett Farm Tobacco Barn, Port Royal, Virginia
Wednesday, April 26, 1865, 5:30AM

Clarkhorn had Corbett accompany him to Atwater's side. Heat from the flaming barn punished them as the General hissed, "You didn't kill him, Sergeant! Damn you for that! You just lost a lifetime supply of money!"

"I need that money and what I see isn't much of a problem, Sir," answered Corbett. "He's bleeding like a stuck pig! It's all over the ground and still gushing. The way he's all twisted up, he looks paralyzed, too. Should I shoot him again, Sir? Is that what you want me to do, Sir?"

"No, you dunce! Over a hundred men and the family are watching and our orders were to bring him in alive unless he endangered me or one of my men. Right now, that bastard couldn't endanger a housefly!" Lemuel looked toward the Garrett's home. "Lay his ass on the porch so nobody can say we did anything else to hurt him. Be sure to raise his feet enough to make him bleed faster."

Corbett needed confirmation. He asked, "Yes, Sir, and Sir, my money...?"

"It's yours if he dies, Sergeant. If he lives, you'll join him..."

32

Richard H. Garrett Farm, Port Royal, Virginia
Wednesday, April 26, 1865, 10AM

No good deed goes unpunished...

Tom watched the soldiers roll Atwater onto his back and tuck a bedroll under his feet. His friend's chest heaved, and a thin red blood line leaked from the corner of Atwater's mouth as he made eye contact with Tom. He mouthed a message only Tom understood.

"I been Judased! They betrayed me like they done Jesus, Tom. They used both of us."

The troopers near Tom couldn't understand their captive's wailing as his everything, his world, his faith, and his love of the Lord, collapsed around him.

33

Senate Office Building, Washington, DC
Thursday, April 27, 1865, 10AM

Washington's ***DAILY MORNING CHRONICLE*** headline trumpeted: 'Booth dead; **accomplice found guilty, will hang today!**' Marilee folded the newspaper to expose the headline before she handed it to Charles.

The senator smiled, read over the fold, and said, "Thank you, my dear! All's well that ends well!" Seeing that she wasn't sharing his smile, he reached into his desk's top right drawer and removed a thick envelope. He extended it to Marilee. She took it, but still didn't smile.

This was new from Marilee. The senator cajoled her, saying, "Come, come, my dear! All is and will be good for us! You are a very wealthy woman." He chuckled. "... And we both know that you love money!"

Marilee opened the envelope. Indeed, she was a very wealthy woman, albeit one who felt more sorrow than anything else. She offered no emotion as she sighed, "That is true, Sir."

The bitch is having a Christian attack, thought Charles. *She could ruin everything! She's smart, beautiful, and useful, but she's no longer dedicated. If she thinks Jesus wants her to turn on me, she'll do it! I don't want to kill her, but I'll be damned if I'll risk my life and fortune!*

She folded her arms across her breasts. "Sir, may I have today off?"

"Of course. Will you be here tomorrow morning?"

"Yes, Sir, if God allows it. If He forgives me…"

"I need to note a reason to pay you for the day. What shall I say?"

Marilee answered, "I'm paving the road to Hell for a man of good intentions."

No further questions followed.

Marilee took her spring jacket from the office hall tree, slipped it on, and left the building.

Moments later, Charles jotted a note to Colonel Elijah Spoon on a piece of stationery, slipped it in an envelope, sealed it, and went downstairs. At the security office, he asked, "Does your book show Colonel Spoon's current location?"

A young sergeant, more clerk than soldier, opened his location log. "Yes, Sir. He has a luncheon engagement with the Colonel's Social Group at Flannery's in Georgetown at noon. He usually arrives a little early for such things."

Charles wrote Elijah Spoon on the envelope and handed it to the sergeant. "I want this waiting for him when he arrives at the restaurant."

34

**Flannery's Restaurant and Hotel, Georgetown,
District of Columbia
Thursday, April 27, 1865, 11:30AM**

The *maître-d hotel* looked up when the bell over the front door tinkled. "Ah, Colonel Spoon," he said. "I got a message for you. It arrived a scant ten minutes ago." He lifted it from his table and extended it. "Your friends are yet to arrive. Please sit anywhere."

Elijah traded the maître-d a silver coin for the envelope and sat near a well-lit window. He recognized Sumner's handwriting as he tore one end away and shook the message free.

He read: ***Send Corbet in civilian dress.***

There was no signature.

35

Senate Office Building, Washington, DC
Wednesday, May 10, 1865, 8:30AM

The Mail Room courier caught Charles Sumner at the top of the stairs. "Senator, this came for you last night. All the way from Brazil, so I thought I'd bring it up first thing; thought it might be something important."

After feigning just enough confusion, Charles accepted the envelope while answering, "Brazil, you say? Can't say that I know anybody who's ever even been there!" After turning the letter over in his hands, he stuck it in his jacket pocket and added with a shrug and a smile, "Oh, well, I get mail from all over... got something from France just last week!"

The mail courier said, "One thing more, Senator. All of us in the mail room were sad to hear what happened to Miss Lewallen. It's hard to believe the stuff that goes on these days!"

"Thank you for those kind words. She was a fine woman," answered Clarkhorn. He excused himself, entered his office, and sat behind his reception desk. His fingers trembled as he tore the envelope's end away and pulled a folded sheet of stationery free.

Charles read: ***Never underestimate hedonism. Glad you're not here.***

There was no signature.

Charles chuckled. "You are one heartless blood sucking son-of-a-bitch, and that's a quality I admire, you broken-legged bastard. I don't miss you, either!"